Software Architecture for Web Developers

An introductory guide for developers striving to take the first steps toward software architecture or just looking to grow as professionals

Mihaela Roxana Ghidersa

BIRMINGHAM—MUMBAI

Software Architecture for Web Developers

Associate Group Product Manager: Pavan Ramchandani
Publishing Product Manager: Aaron Tanna
Senior Editor: Aamir Ahmed
Content Development Editor: Divya Vijayan
Technical Editor: Simran Udasi
Copy Editor: Safis Editing
Project Coordinator: Sonam Pandey
Proofreader: Safis Editing
Indexer: Rekha Nair
Production Designer: Roshan Kawale
Marketing Coordinators: Anamika Singh and Marylou De Mello

First published: October 2022
Production reference: 1230922

Published by Packt Publishing Ltd.
Livery Place
35 Livery Street
Birmingham
B3 2PB, UK.

ISBN 978-1-80323-791-6

www.packt.com

"How long can you afford to put off who you really want to be? Your nobler self cannot wait any longer. Decide to be extraordinary and do what you need to do now." - Epictetus

Contributors

About the author

Mihaela Roxana Ghidersa is a software developer who has a passion for technology. She enjoys building and delivering quality while trying to have fun as much as possible. She is willing to learn from others and share her knowledge, which has guided her to become a Microsoft MVP. She has been raised professionally by the community through conferences, training, and sessions, and she is trying to pay it forward by speaking at conferences, writing, and mentoring. She is perceptive and innovative, not afraid to exploit her best version and go the extra mile outside her conventional comfort zone. This exact desire to get out of her comfort zone has led her in recent years to switch from full-stack, frontend API design to technical leadership and architecture.

To everyone who inspired me and gave me the courage to be more. Thank you.
I'm still learning.

About the reviewer

Daniele Serfilippi is a senior software engineer and architect with decades of experience in designing and building enterprise-level web applications. His passion and dedication have led him to important roles such as head of engineering and deputy CTO at international companies. He's also an instructor, mentor, content creator, and community builder. He shares content daily with his tens of thousands of followers about software engineering, software architecture, and the JavaScript ecosystem.

His continuous learning mindset constantly drives him to improve his skill set, experiment with new technologies, and explore new fields, such as machine learning, blockchain, and Web3.

His mission: design apps that improve and empower people's lives.

Table of Contents

7

Leveraging Soft Skills   73

Part 3 – From Developer to Architect

8

Who Codes and Who "Architects"?   83

9

Break the Rules   89

Preface

This book came from a need I had at the beginning of my career: the need to know what it means to build a product from a high level to the details. Web developers often limit themselves to the daily job of coding. They start looking at the application architecture, design, and evolution only if they are lucky enough to find good mentors or the right circumstances in the company that encourage them to grow. I want this book to bring value to every web developer who wants to go to the next level in their career and to be their go-to guide.

Who this book is for

I intend to create a guide for both web developers that aspire for an architect role and web developers that, even though they are not pursuing such a role, want to become better professionals and understand the role and impact of good architecture in their projects.

If you are an architect, I hope that after reading this book, you reconsider the relationship with the development team. If you are a developer, I hope that between the pages of this book, you find knowledge, business insights, technical best practices, and ideas that will push you to improve your work.

What this book covers

Chapter 1, *The Role of Architecture*, looks at how, day by day, we do our tasks without realizing that we are building toward architecture. We need to understand how many benefits good architecture brings and how damaging lousy architecture can be. What is the impact of architecture on the other stakeholders besides the development team? We bring light to all these matters from the beginning.

Chapter 2, *Diving into Some Common Architectural Patterns*, discusses how no matter whether we are in the early years of our career or pursuing a career as an architect, as long as we build an application, we need to understand what we are building, what patterns we are creating, and why some decisions were made. This chapter covers some of the most common architectural patterns.

Chapter 3, *Myths about Architecture*, destroys some of the myths that web developers meet or create along the way regarding the architect and the architecture.

Chapter 4, *Discussing What Good Architecture Is*, covers some essential characteristics of good architecture. We will explain them one by one using relevant examples.

Chapter 5, *Design versus Architecture*, compares and explains an application's architecture and design since we often confuse them. We will also point out how they work together.

Chapter 6, Types of Software Architects and Their Focus, divides and discusses different types of architecture and architects depending on their focus and level: for example, business, tech, or combined.

Chapter 7, Leveraging Soft Skills, focuses on the primary soft skills we need to develop to do a great job as an architect and meet all the requirements. Having a role where you interact with so many stakeholders creates a great need to develop skills such as time management, prioritization, communication, and so on.

Chapter 8, Who Codes and Who "Architects"?, focuses on collaboration. Whether we talk about collaboration at the business level or in the team, or about experienced web developers, juniors, architects, or technical leads, the application is built by working together and collaborating.

Chapter 9, Break the Rules, discusses self-discipline and engagement in the process. We will also open the discussion about software craftsmanship and related principles that help a web developer become an expert.

Download the color images

We also provide a PDF file that has color images of the screenshots and diagrams used in this book. You can download it here: `https://packt.link/p3YMu`.

Conventions used

There are a number of text conventions used throughout this book.

Bold: Indicates a new term, an important word, or words that you see onscreen. For instance, words in menus or dialog boxes appear in **bold**. Here is an example: "Select **System info** from the **Administration** panel."

> **Tips or Important Notes**
> Appear like this.

Get in touch

Feedback from our readers is always welcome.

General feedback: If you have questions about any aspect of this book, email us at `customercare@packtpub.com` and mention the book title in the subject of your message.

Errata: Although we have taken every care to ensure the accuracy of our content, mistakes do happen. If you have found a mistake in this book, we would be grateful if you would report this to us. Please visit `www.packtpub.com/support/errata` and fill in the form.

Piracy: If you come across any illegal copies of our works in any form on the internet, we would be grateful if you would provide us with the location address or website name. Please contact us at copyright@packt.com with a link to the material.

If you are interested in becoming an author: If there is a topic that you have expertise in and you are interested in either writing or contributing to a book, please visit authors.packtpub.com.

Share Your Thoughts

Once you've read *Software Architecture for Web Developers*, we'd love to hear your thoughts! Scan the QR code below to go straight to the Amazon review page for this book and share your feedback.

https://packt.link/r/1803237910

Your review is important to us and the tech community and will help us make sure we're delivering excellent quality content.

Part 1 – Getting the Grasp of Architecture

Upon completing this part, you will have a more precise understanding of the architecture's role, its impact at all levels, and who the stakeholders are.

This part comprises the following chapters:

- *Chapter 1, The Role of Architecture*
- *Chapter 2, Diving into Some Common Architectural Patterns*
- *Chapter 3, Myths about Architecture*
- *Chapter 4, Discussing What Good Architecture Is*
- *Chapter 5, Design versus Architecture*

1
The Role of Architecture

The tech stage has erupted in the last decade. We now work on some of the most complex systems ever. As users, we need the flows in our applications to be fast. Almost all our actions happen on our phones or online, from socializing and entertaining ourselves to paying bills and making medical appointments. At the same time, many of the applications we use are monetized, so we need features to create the best content. On the other hand, from the cars we drive to the houses we build, everything has some features that implement AI, IoT, or some kind of application that automates specific actions. From the database to the code, from functionality and user interaction to how systems are organized, we are faced with challenges at every step in the development process of a product. More than ever, it is essential to understand what we have, what we can build with our information, and what our end goal is. This is how the need for a structure arose, and it became increasingly important to create systems that could evolve while maintaining the balance between business and tech requirements.

In this chapter, we will cover the following topics:

- What is architecture and why is it so important?
- The impact of architecture
- Understanding the role of stakeholders

What is architecture and why is it so important?

If you ask a group of developers what kind of architecture works for them, you will receive many different responses reflecting each person's experience. Architecture is a term used to define many structures, but we often hear about it within the construction domain. The parallel here extends beyond the use of the noun itself to the common fact that, as we will discuss in *Chapter 5, Design versus Architecture*, structure, and design, whether for software or a building, are the results of the requirements of different stakeholders.

Explaining precisely what software architecture is or does is hard. Still, luckily, an at-hand comparison that gives us some perspective on the impact of an architectural decision is building architecture. Just think about how hard it is to change the architecture of a finished construction. The same goes for software. Even if the "damage" is not as visible as it would be when tearing a house apart and building it again, the implications are the same: time, finances, and an impact on different areas and stakeholders.

Can we define software architecture?

The debate always comes down to one question: "*What is software architecture?*" Although it is a highly discussed and important matter, there is no definitive and generally applicable definition. While trying to shape a meaning as thoroughly as possible, I have found many interpretations and explanations, many confusing and hard to tackle, while others were simple and to the point. For me, the subject of architecture started to make sense when I started working on a project as a full-stack developer. As I had to go through different layers in the application (working from the database to the client), I had to respect the rules that this architecture imposed. Then, step by step, by becoming more curious about different technologies and approaches in other projects, I discovered that this is an exciting and essential matter that I had to explore fully. So, to gain some clarity, let's take the first step by discussing some existing definitions and perspectives, and then we will try to shape a report.

According to Ralph Johnson, "*architecture is about the important stuff. Whatever that is.*" This is a very abstract definition but may be a good representation of how important the context of the project is when determining the architecture.

Another exciting perspective I found from Eoin Woods states that "*software architecture is the set of design decisions that, if made incorrectly, may cause your project to be canceled.*" Though radical, Eoin Woods' definition exemplifies how important it is to always ensure we have explicit requirements when making decisions about a system's structure.

The list of examples can go on; however, my conclusion was that many seemed pretty abstract and ambiguous for a developer, especially one in the early years of their career. From "*the process of defining a structured solution that meets all of the technical and operational requirements*" to "*the set of structures needed to reason about the system, which comprises software elements, relations among them, and properties of both*," each of them yet again simply underline my idea that defining architecture would create constraints and possibly many debates. What if software architecture is a set of characteristics to pay attention to while expressing a direction on which we build step by step?

From my experience, the simplest way to think about software architecture, no matter the level of experience, is this:

Software architecture is a set of characteristics that combine technical and business requirements (at the project and organization levels). You will be able to define a skeleton to help you build a performant, secure, and easy-to-extend system (or application).

So, it is a structure upon which we build step by step, one component after another, creating the relationships between them. Consider that all this is being realized while considering the bigger picture of the product.

Even though we talk about components and interactions, we must be careful with the level of abstraction. We can quickly get too absorbed in the implementation details and lose our view from where we are to where we want to go within our application development map. There is a fine line between software development and software architecture. In my opinion, and from the experiences I've had within the teams I've had the chance to interact with, I can say that it is obvious when an architect is too focused on abstractions and has no idea about what is happening in the application. At the same time, I can see when a developer lacks awareness of the software architecture.

We will debate an architect's involvement in the development process in *Chapter 6, Types of Architects and Their Focus*. That's why right now, I would like us to focus a bit more on how software architecture knowledge can help us write better code.

Among all the questions we address when talking about software architecture, two can significantly help in the development process: "*What are the main components the application can be divided into?*" and "*How do these components share responsibility?*"

Understanding how the system is divided into components and how they interact brings much greater clarity to the process of defining the responsibilities of each, seeing where best practices integrate, bringing value to reduce the interdependence of different parts of the code, and easing the process of creating unit tests. At the same time, we have a huge advantage because it will become easier to identify frequently used components, create a common ground, and apply the correct patterns.

It is easier to respect best practices and choose suitable design patterns and abstractions when we understand what we are building and why certain decisions were made at the architecture level. Everything works together beautifully and we find it easier to build a quality-oriented product (a product that respects the quality attributes set at the birth of the product).

Understanding that my team needs an overview of the application's architecture was a stepping point in reconsidering how certain pieces of the system interact. This is extremely useful, mainly when we discuss complex team organization with dedicated subteams. It's hard to keep track of how all the components interact, define precise requirements (especially for the teams we are dependent on), and create pieces of components that fit together when there is no overview.

All in all, if the structure of the system is built the right way, we will have a successful product. If not, at some point, we will have to start over or rewrite essential parts.

When I'm referring to the base, I particularly consider two directions:

- Architecture is the foundation of the application. We already discussed this; it is as though we were building a house. It has to allow you to create the walls, the roof later, and other details that you might want along the way or as trends evolve and change, but above all, it should give stability and direction for how the rest will grow at a structural level. The architecture is a system's base and must be carefully thought through to bypass any significant design changes and code refactoring later.

- On the other side, the development team is also the base. We can have the best architecture plan, but if the ones building it step by step don't know what they're supposed to be doing or don't have an overview to support this, we will come into a lot of trouble.

A slight improvement at the code level to support the system's architecture or design will have a considerable impact over time.

An important aspect to consider when it comes to architecture is the fact that it has to be shaped around requirements of significant impact. Good architecture is not one with fixed definitions and limits but one in which technical needs and business requirements are aligned and work well together. I was part of a team where the development team was composed of great developers, but the requirements were dramatically changing, and this made it hard to have continuity in the product life cycle. We had to constantly change the structure, rewrite parts, and had a lot of technical debt to take care of.

Another critical aspect is that the architecture should focus on the high-level structure, independent of the implementation details. Of course, implementation details are being decided along the way and are not to be ignored, but they shouldn't impact the structure; instead, they should build upon the structure.

From the start, it is essential to know that we have to be as pragmatic as possible and consider as many scenarios as we can when deciding the architectural shape. Since we are discussing strategies and edge cases, an excellent way of being as precise as possible about these is by exploring and analyzing the future steps and plans with the stakeholders. Stakeholders are critical and of great help in building a valuable product by providing feedback. In the *Understanding the role of stakeholders* section of this chapter, we will discuss the main stakeholders and why they impact the application.

So, we agreed that it is hard to define architecture, and we saw that what needs attention is determined by the context of the product you are building. At the same time, even though we can provide a clear definition, we can still learn best from the experience of others and look at some points that, in time, show themselves to be of great value.

Requirements

Often, we might feel as though architecture is all about technical requirements and concerns, but the actual value of a project is given by the functional requirements and the validation of stakeholders. You can have the technically best product with the best architecture and components, but if no one uses it, all that effort is in vain. One of the best skills an architect can build is balancing the functional and non-functional requirements.

Working closely with the various stakeholders as possible helps us correctly identify, understand, and refine our requirements. Ultimately, the end software architecture solution will be defined by those requirements. This is part of the context we have already mentioned. Suppose the system architecture is defined too much by the business context and we make a choice that cannot meet all requirements. In that case, we will end up with anything but a solid architecture that can later be extended or even implemented.

Maintainability and extensibility

System maintainability is the subject of many books but is still very subjectively defined in many cases. This property determines how easily you can change, refactor, extend, or repair your software. Software maintenance is an ongoing process, so it's essential to be prepared to use the least amount of resources possible to make this possible.

Your architecture should be flexible enough to allow you to work with requirements later that you were not aware of in the beginning. As an architect, even if you don't have 100% of the details in place, to be safe, you have to at least think in terms of the evolution of your system. Predict possible risks and find ways to avoid them.

But I have a disclaimer here, which also applies in the development process: don't over-engineer scenarios if you don't know whether they will ever even happen. When I mention that we need to prepare for change, I refer to respecting best practices, making the code easy to work with, and extending and modifying, rather than predicting what might happen in the future. Here, we can turn to the **You Ain't Gonna Need It (YAGNI)** concept, which represents incrementally creating a simple system design. When you find yourself saying, "*Maybe the client, user, or product owner will want this functionality in the future, so I will also code for that scenario*," stop for a second, and acknowledge that you are overthinking and that you're about to code for a scenario that will never happen. Instead, evaluate how testable, clean, and extendable your code is and move on.

Response to change

As business evolves, so does software; it is a natural consequence. Technology evolves, business perspectives change, technical debt appears, requirements are reconsidered, team structures change, and the need for a more performant technology stack arises. What we need is to think in terms of building tolerance to change in the system. Observe where and what kind of changes appear through iterations. You can expect these changes and be prepared to meet them. Why so much analysis? Because every time we assume a final decision, we are also saying no to other details we might receive along the way, which will help us make a more informed decision. Once you have committed to a way of shaping your architecture, you have already decided how the next period of time will be spent and how the product and the architectural structure will evolve.

James Clear aptly defines the importance of decision-making by stating that *"when you say no, you are only saying no to one option. When you say yes, you are saying no to every other option. No is a decision. Yes, it is a responsibility. Be careful what (and who) you say yes to. It will shape your day, career, family, life."* This is also valid when it comes to software development decisions.

Take care of how the pieces of the system interact, reduce complexity and independence as much as possible, and identify the essential components and how they are being implemented. This way, even if you have to change something along the way, the changes will be isolated, and a complete architectural remake can be avoided.

Practicality

Defining architecture is not just a preliminary stage; it is a continuous process. In this case, the architect is responsible for having a clear perspective on how the system evolves and if the decisions made at the beginning are still valid. At the same time, the software architect must ensure that everyone on board understands how the system works. Whether we like it or not, systems become more complex as they evolve. This complexity can sometimes be hard to observe or tackle early on. When we start losing our understanding of what we are building, we end up with a huge problem. As the system becomes harder to understand, it becomes tedious to reuse some parts, stick to the design decisions, maintain it, or extend it. As the team structure changes, the learning curve for new members increases.

Looking back at the history of software architecture, we notice a shift in creating this timeline of decisions. In the beginning, architectural decisions were, without exception, made in the early development stage, seen as important and hard-to-change decisions. Later, with the rise of agile and the philosophy of working with iterations and being open to change, the approach changed, and the conclusion reached was that the process of shaping a system should be smooth and in sync with change. So, the emphasis was placed on how open to change, extensible, and maintainable the system was in reality.

Quality attributes

Let's say we defined and agreed upon requirements with the stakeholders; so, what's next? Another significant step that needs to be done as early as possible in the life cycle of a product is considering quality attributes. You know you have explicit quality attributes when they shine through the application. You don't have to wait for it to be developed or deployed; the architecture should speak for itself. By defining quality attributes, we become more particular about whether we can meet all the requirements or not. For example, by thinking about performance at every step of extending the system, we end up with a performant application because, for example, we will consider what change detectors we have from the perspective of a frontend developer, in the client and where, how many times we load a page, or how many calls an API can handle. A quality attribute guides us. Later, it might become complex and time-consuming to make impactful decisions and changes in these areas.

The product quality model defined in ISO/IEC 25010 comprises the eight quality characteristics shown in the following figure:

Figure 1.1– Quality model (source: https://iso25000.com/)

Next, we will discuss how architecture is more than technical decisions and how considering the context in which we build the product will help us make better decisions.

The impact of architecture

The architectural decisions are those that you can't reverse without some degree of effort. Or, simply put, they're the things that you find hard to refactor in an afternoon.
- Simon Brown

Because we can't change an architectural decision in an afternoon, the first step in architecting software is understanding what is significant and why. When talking about substantial matters, we talk about concepts such as the technologies chosen or the high-level structure, understanding how to tackle risks, and controlling the complexity we add to the big picture as we make changes. An excellent example of a significant decision I had to work with was how to switch some applications from AngularJS to the new Angular when AngularJS became unable to comply with certain UI or UX requirements. Or, when perspective changes were made, many applications wanted to break the monolith and switch to a microservices-oriented architecture. These are changes that need a high degree of effort and resources.

It's easy to think that if you are writing good code and following some well-tested approaches, keeping an eye on the architecture is not essential. However, there are some benefits to getting the bigger picture, from understanding how components in the system should interact to which should have what responsibility and the cost of what you are implementing as a developer. Having an overview of the architectural dynamics helps us answer radical questions such as the following:

- Which are the main components of my system?

- How do these components interact and evolve?

- What resources will I need and what costs will I have in the development process?

- What are the areas where I can predict change?

Another important metric is the ability to predict change. Darwin's theory says that the species that survives is not the strongest but the one that adapts better to change. If Darwin had worked in software development, I think he would have stated that the system that survives longer is not the strongest but the one that has an architect that can predict and adapt better to change.

Often, we encounter the idea that development teams should focus their attention on coding and not bother with architectural concepts since those aren't their primary concern. This is an incorrect way of looking at things because there are so many benefits to looking at what you are working on from above. For example, the moment I stepped away from the IDE because things were not making sense, I started to understand what I was building and came up with better solutions instead of complaining about the same problems I didn't understand before. Working toward consistency between the process of translating features to code and the process of defining best practices, I could see where some technical guidance might be needed and visualize component interactions from a higher level. It changed my perspective on my daily work.

Development-level benefits

I firmly believe that the architect's perspective can be flawless. Still, if the team implementing the architecture does not understand what they are building, that is a big red flag regarding the team dynamics.

Some of the matters that improve at the development level when creating an overview of what we are building are as follows:

- *Consistency regarding the way we implement features*: align when starting to work on a new part, have knowledge-sharing sessions if needed, undertake pair programming, and brainstorm how to solve certain problems.

- *Consistency regarding code quality*: everyone should be aware of the guidelines and best practices and apply them consistently to grow a healthy system.

- *It's easier to evaluate the team technically*: when we know the practices we follow and test, it is easier to spot the areas where something is not okay. It is easy to note in the team when and if someone does not understand what they have to do.

- *It's easier to identify the specific points where technical leadership is necessary*.

- *Same overview and vision*: the whole team works toward the same objectives when the objectives are clear.

- *Validation for the whole structure*: architecture is being implemented through code. If we don't write quality code backed up by best practices, the consequences will be reflected in how the architecture evolves or can't evolve. The reverse is also valid. Best practices and excellent developers can't do much with bad architecture. Potentially reuse some parts when rewriting. It is healthy to identify this kind of matter, align, and have everyone on the same page.

We understand how all the pieces work together, how they will evolve in relationship with one another, and why it is essential to respect quality guidelines. At the same time, the team is motivated to work on themselves and improve their skills to build a high-quality product.

Application-level benefits

When discussing requirements, there will always be a definitive list of what people want a system to do. Alongside this, a plan split nicely between features, user stories, flows, and even tasks will always exist.

Some requirements are not understood very well and are requested just because they are popular in the market. We don't know what they mean in detail in terms of implementation, but we know they are essential for "performance" or "security." I have seen this situation in architecture workshops. When talking about the well-known "quality attributes," everyone wants them, but they aren't all equally important in the product context. They are, at the same time, hard to implement all at once, and they must be prioritized. It is like someone saying that from today on, they will exercise daily, eat healthily, read 50 pages, and meditate. It's impossible to enact all of this at once. You need to take it step by step, see what impacts your life most, and add more improvements along the way. The same goes for architectural quality attributes. We need to check the most important ones, how they influence each other, and what metrics we need to ensure they have the desired results and impact.

Some are more relevant and have more weight depending on the context of your system. One of the best approaches when you don't know what you want from a system is to list what you don't want.

Some results of bad decisions could be the following:

- **Complexity** – your system is hard to work with, hard to understand, and hard to explain. Always check that the code you write is easy to understand and that the design and architectural decisions you make are clear to everyone involved in the development process. Make the system easy to understand.

- **Not being able to test** – if you can't test your system, it's because you have too much coupling or some of your components do too much. Create modularity so that your layers and components can change independently without impacting other parts. Create tests to track when changes negatively impact other areas. Also, if you want to extend the system without testing it at every change, having considerable coverage is a safety net.

- **Unmaintainable and hard to extend** – this is a toxic circle. An untested system is a system predisposed to increasing complexity; complexity makes the system hard to understand, so it becomes tough to extend, maintain, or even refactor.

- **Fragility** – with every new thing you add or fix, something that seems completely unrelated breaks. This makes it very hard to be productive, takes a lot of time to investigate, and takes a lot of testing to gain back some control.

We will go into further detail about the approaches, principles, and ways of controlling the quality of our architecture in *Chapter 4, Discussing What Good Architecture Is*, but first, it's essential to give some shape to the way architectural components should interact and evolve by discussing some of the must-know principles of every developer: the SOLID principles.

SOLID represents an acronym for some of the most popular design principles. These principles can be implemented at any level of code complexity and are intended to make software maintainable, extendable, flexible, and testable. The principles were promoted by Robert C. Martin (Uncle Bob) in his 2000 paper, *Design Principles and Design Patterns*. The SOLID acronym was introduced later by Michael Feathers.

Uncle Bob is also well known as the author of *Clean Code* and *Clean Architecture*, so these principles are strongly tied to clean coding, clean architecture, and quality patterns.

One of the main benefits of these five principles is that they help us to see the need for specific design patterns and software architecture in general. So, I believe that this is a topic that every developer should learn about.

Let's look at the five principles in detail:

- Single Responsibility principle
- Open-Closed principle
- Liskov Substitution principle
- Interface Segregation principle
- Dependency Inversion principle

Single-Responsibility principle

"There should never be more than one reason for a class to change. In other words, every type should have only one responsibility."

The first principle refers to the fact that each component, at any level – including the architectural level – should be thought of as having only one responsibility, one unique matter to resolve, and a single reason to change. This principle also represents massive support for the maintenance process because it helps with the following:

- Avoiding coupling. Coupling indicates how dependent on or independent of one another components are. High coupling is an issue.
- Creating small, independent structures that are easier to test.
- Shaping a system that is easier to read and understand.

Open-Closed principle

"Software entities ... should be open for extension but closed for modification."

The systems we build are ever-changing due to shifting requirements and technological evolution. Having to deal with so much change and having to extend or maintain systems helps us along the way to gain experience and lessons to make better future products. One of the lessons is precisely what this principle stands for: entities and components should be independent enough so that if the need for change appears in the future, the impact on existing structures is as minimal as possible.

Liskov Substitution principle

"Functions that use pointers or references to base classes must be able to use objects of derived classes without knowing it."

This principle is one of the hardest to understand, but we will dig deeper into the technical details later. For now, and in the context of architecture components, let's keep in mind that this principle simply requires that every derived component should be substitutable for its parent component.

Interface Segregation principle

"Many client-specific interfaces are better than one general-purpose interface."

The I in SOLID stands for more than the I in Interface – it stands for an attitude, a skill that comes with experience. This principle states that we should always be careful and split significant components or interfaces into smaller ones. This principle works very well with the S from SOLID because we can determine whether an element has more than one responsibility and needs splitting.

Dependency Inversion principle

"Depend upon abstractions, [not] concretions."

The principle of dependency inversion refers to the decoupling of software modules. Understanding this principle is valuable because it helps us to see abstractions. High-level components should not depend on low-level features; both should depend on abstractions. As a result, the changes we make in the higher-level components won't impact the implementation details.

Understanding the role of stakeholders

Being part of the team and being focused on development can take the focus away from who is impacted by our work. We talk so much about user needs and experience that we cannot look from above and see all the parts affected by our product. Until the moment of being used, systems must be shaped, built and tested, may have to be extended, and are usually maintained, planned, and financed.

The truth is that stakeholders have a great deal of decisional impact on the product's evolution and we must pay attention to their needs. The stakeholders are the ones from whom the demand for a product appears. You must identify your stakeholders, keep them close, understand their needs and perspectives, and create an architecture that meets their requirements as effectively as possible.

Software development, and software architecture even more so, can become very complex. Also, as we already discussed, software architecture is tremendously impacted by requirements, and those requirements come from people that are not necessarily technically minded; so, in this case, it is an architect's job to make sure that everyone understands what we are building. This way, we ensure everyone knows the product's direction and structure and can keep track of its evolution and changes. Having everyone on the same page can provide valuable feedback and help us make better-informed decisions.

When thinking about stakeholders, we can use this classification to identify them quickly:

- Before getting to the users, analyze who is part of building the product, such as the project management team, development team, and designers.

- Look at who is using your product, such as the customers and users.

- There are also people not directly involved and not using the product but who are part of the process by facilitating some actions and techniques, such as top managers and company owners.

Summary

Software architecture is a set of characteristics that combines both the technical and business requirements, with which we will be able to define a skeleton that will help us to build a performant, secure, and easily extendable system.

Software architecture is not a one-time decision but a part of a continuous process.

A successful architecture builds a system used in real-life scenarios by real users and is validated by all relevant stakeholders. You can have the best system technically, but if it does not fulfill the needs of stakeholders, your effort is in vain.

Stakeholders are not only just users and should be part of the architecting process. Identify stakeholders, try to understand what they need, define the precise requirements, and implement them using quality attributes.

The next chapter will examine some popular patterns used in defining the architecture.

2

Diving into Some Common Architectural Patterns

In the previous chapter, we recognized the importance of software changes and will extend the discussion on how we should respond to these changes later in the book. The good thing is that we also learned how to work with existing approaches and patterns in the present context, alongside the evolution of requirements. If we were to open a forum on API design and architecture, we would find many discussions around the monolith. We now seek to decompose applications into more minor, decentralized services.

When discussing technical solutions, the truth is that there is no silver bullet. We must research and learn about the best options to fit our needs. When talking about new approaches and technologies, we need to understand that time will tell whether they are trustworthy and on which kinds of systems they work best. As a result, these new patterns bring many challenges and shifts in mindset. From state management and asynchronous operations to complex deployments and more robust monitoring of systems, there are many factors to consider and new approaches to understand.

There are given steps to follow when starting to work on a system's architecture, from asking yourself what kind of architecture you want to build to what kind of technologies, patterns, and principles you want to use.

We'll cover the following main topics in this chapter:

- Architectural patterns
- Architectural style versus architectural patterns
- Common patterns:
    - The layered pattern
    - The client-server pattern
    - The model-view-controller pattern

- The microservices pattern
- The CQRS pattern
- UI patterns (Micro frontends, Flux, and Jamstack)

Architectural patterns

Architectural patterns determine the later constraints in many areas, from design to how we deploy a solution. It is essential to research and make sure we make an informed decision. An architectural pattern shapes our system and determines how high-level elements will evolve and interact with one another. Also, as we discussed regarding decision-making in the previous chapter, an architectural pattern will give us direction and make it easier to predict any future concerns or risks. Finally, although for a long time, the feeling was that developers shouldn't be so concerned about the architecture, our choice in terms of architecture will influence design patterns, principles, and approaches that will make development easier.

On the other hand, I think it is essential to make this disclaimer: there is no entirely bad or good pattern. All of them have benefits and costs. Based on the specific context, a particular choice will create challenges, or it might bring complexity. It is a matter of making the choices that cost you the least and benefit you the most.

The good part is that we don't have to reinvent the wheel. There are already a lot of tested patterns that we can choose from, to begin with. We have to set some objectives regarding quality attributes such as performance, scalability, and security – and don't forget about deployability. The approach you use when it comes to delivery has to be efficient.

Choice of technology

Once we decide what pattern we will follow in terms of architecture, the next step is to determine which technologies we will implement. To make the best choices, it's a great advantage to have experience with a wide range of technologies and understand their inner workings, pros, and cons. Also, as the tech stack is evolving rapidly, it is good to stay up to date to make the best decisions on the frameworks and libraries that will complement your architecture.

Quality patterns

The whole journey of shaping architecture aims to check as many requirements as possible, both technically and functionally. We must ensure we know which quality characteristics will be the main ones in our software product's development.

ISO/IEC 25010 defines these requirements as follows:

> *"The quality of a system is the degree to which the system satisfies the stated and implied needs of its various stakeholders and thus provides value. Those stakeholders' needs (functionality, performance, security, maintainability, etc.) are precisely what is represented in the quality model, which categorizes the product quality into characteristics and sub-characteristics."*

So, let's look at how each requirement is being defined and try to see how they fit together and in which contexts:

- **Functional suitability** – This characteristic demonstrates the level to which a product or system provides the functions that meet the stated and implied needs when used under specified conditions

- **Performance efficiency** – This characteristic reflects the performance based on the number of resources used under stated conditions

- **Compatibility** – The level to which one product, system, or component can exchange information with other products, systems, or components, and still perform its required functions while sharing the same hardware or software environment

- **Usability** – In a specific context, we check whether a product or system can be used by specific users to achieve specific goals with effectiveness, efficiency, and satisfaction

- **Reliability** – Here, we check whether a system, product, or component can perform the specified functions under specified conditions for a specified time period

- **Security** – Next, we check whether a product or system protects information and data to the desired level so that other products, systems, or people have data access appropriate to their level of authorization

- **Maintainability** – Next, we check the level of effectiveness and efficiency with which a product or system can be modified so it can improve, correct, or adapt to the changes in the environment and the requirements

- **Portability** – Lastly, we check whether a system, product, or component from one hardware, software, or other operational or usage environment can be effectively and efficiently transferred to another

Each of these characteristics will translate into a specific approach depending on the system's needs. Still, it is important to prioritize them and measure whether they are followed, if so, how, and that everyone involved in the development process is on the same page.

Where did it all start?

Just as in building architecture, a pattern captures a group of design principles and elements that make software reusable. We encounter issues we've worked on before and apply the exact solutions to our work. This happens to developers from different teams and companies all around the world. This is precisely how patterns appear, from the need to reuse solutions to recurring problems in the systems we work with. The beautiful part about understanding and using specific practices is that we can use the same patterns even if we change teams or companies. From my experience, having at least some awareness of architectural or design patterns helps us be more efficient in our work and understand a new code base more quickly.

I have a close friend who is an architect, and I'm interested in software architecture enough to research often how buildings, communities, people, and software are related. That's how I stumbled upon two books that got my attention, and I would like to share some of their ideas with you. The books are *A Timeless Way of Building* and *A Pattern Language* by Christopher Alexander.

Christopher Alexander is an architect, builder, and design theorist whose ideas about how people should design houses and communities for themselves have affected fields beyond architecture, including software. He is also known as the father of the pattern language movement.

What caught my attention is that some ideas about design patterns for architecture presented by Christopher Alexander were adapted to software engineering by Kent Beck and Ward Cunningham. They wrote their first design pattern for designing user interfaces. Later on, Erich Gamma and his colleagues, known as the **Gang of Four** (**GoF**), published *Design Patterns: Elements of Reusable Object-Oriented Software*, which made the patterns we so often go to when we need to decompose complex structures familiar in an approachable way (source: `https://hillside.net/patterns/about-patterns`).

In his book *A Pattern Language*, Christopher Alexander explained that "each pattern describes a problem which occurs over and over again in our environment, and then describes the core of the solution to that problem, in a way that you can use this solution a million times over, without ever doing it the same way twice."

And this is precisely how we should approach software architecture. If I have these requirements and this set of quality attributes, what is the solution that satisfies this situation the best? In essence, patterns are a way to gather specific approaches, best practices, and principles, and combine them in a way that makes them easy to reuse. Many applications, at their core, try to resolve similar issues in different contexts or solve various problems in a standard way. So, why reinvent the wheel when some excellent wheel makers have defined these approaches, tested them over time by other teams, and polished them to the extent that they are now part of a common language?

I think learning old computer science wisdom from other developers' experiences is essential. This way, we achieve tech evolution and build better products. For me, learning from the experience of others was a way to grow. I learned from others' mistakes, articles, and books and watched conferences to get the not-so-official version of the story. I'm always curious about the inner workings of every tool and approach, so I always ask questions about how that approach could go wrong and why. After all, I try to look at a solution as best I can with a critical eye to ensure I consider all sides of the story.

Always question everything, take it with a grain of salt, and consider how you would approach the problem if you had to make a particular decision.

Architectural style versus architectural patterns

Because we need to understand and question everything, it is crucial to discuss software architectural patterns and how they differ from architectural styles.

Architectural styles

Defined most simply, an architectural style represents a combination of design decisions and principles to organize our application and code in a certain way. It is the highest level of organization, not used to solve a problem but to enhance certain good practices in a particular type of system.

Of course, we can mix different styles based on our needs and create a custom style for what we want to achieve.

Architectural patterns

An architectural pattern is a group of architectural decisions and principles applied in different contexts to resolve any repeating issues. Long story short, an architectural pattern is a way of solving a recurring architectural problem.

Ultimately, an architectural pattern can represent a solution used in a particular architectural style for a specific problem regarding the relationships between components and how the different layers communicate.

Suppose we were to define a relationship between architectural styles and architectural patterns. In that case, we could say that an architectural pattern describes a solution for any issues related to how we are trying to implement an architectural style.

Sometimes, it can be hard to differentiate between them or have the best view from the top of what approach should be used, so it is crucial to start step by step.

Be sure you understand and are aware of some of the most critical crosscutting concerns, such as the following:

- Performance
- Security
- Logging

- Communication

- Deployment

- Maintainability

- Scalability

- Monitoring

- Usability

Then ask yourself some questions, such as *"What issues does my choice of pattern address?"*, *"How should my modules interact to create a structure as efficiently as possible?"*, and *"How do my technical mindset and decisions influence nontechnical requirements and structures, and the other way around?"*.

There is a great quote from Abraham Lincoln that shares the mindset we should embrace when deciding on architectural patterns: *"Give me six hours to chop down a tree, and I will spend the first four sharpening the ax."* Don't rush into implementing your first idea; know your context, stakeholders, quality attributes, and crosscutting concerns, and then pick the tool closest to what you want to achieve. Let's look at some tools and approaches that we might consider.

Common patterns

As we mentioned before, we don't have to create a new architectural pattern every time we start working on a new system. There are a lot of already-tested and well-documented architectural patterns and approaches that we can begin with. An important aspect to consider is that you can combine techniques if it suits your system, but please be careful because you can quickly end up with a mess if you are not careful.

Some of the patterns that we will look at in this section are the following:

- The layered pattern

- The client-server pattern

- The model-view-controller pattern

- The microservices pattern

- The CQRS pattern

- UI patterns:

  - Micro frontends

  - Flux

  - Jamstack

The layered pattern

One of the first architectural patterns I ever worked with was the layered pattern, also known as the n-tier pattern. The layered pattern is also one of the easiest to understand, especially for developers at the beginning of their career, because it works with different levels of abstraction in terms of how these layers communicate. At the same time, each layer has a very well-defined role and strict interaction rules with the others.

A layered approach best suits applications with a strong focus on testability because it facilitates decoupling and provides independent units. The way this pattern is organized gives us the freedom to use a customizable number of layers, but the most famous structure is composed of four tiers (*Figure 2.1*):

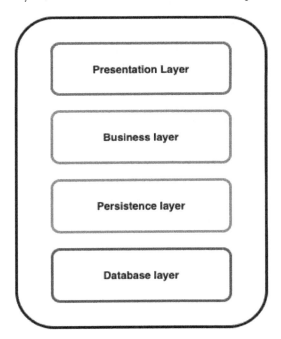

Figure 2.1 – The basic structure of the layered pattern

- Presentation layer (UI layer) – This contains all categories related to the presentation. Users interact with the application through this layer using screens, forms, menus, and reports.
- Business layer – This is where all the business logic lies.
- Persistence layer – This layer handles mapping functions and other operations.
- Database layer – This is the place where all the data is stored.

Besides the organization depending on the primary concern of each layer, another aspect of this pattern is that these layers interact in a unidirectional pattern. So, the organization of this pattern is easy to understand and helps developers write code in a structured way.

Drawbacks

If a small number of layers is easy to follow and implement, the more layers we add, the more the complexity starts to grow because it can become hard to follow each purpose when we are splitting things up.

Also, the performance of this pattern can decrease when the number of layers increases because it is inefficient to go through multiple layers of the architecture, and it might not be feasible, especially for simple operations.

As a result, a good approach would be to keep a smaller number of layers and use this pattern for systems that don't have complex operations to fulfill. This is a good option if you want to build a small application in a relatively short time.

The client-server pattern

The client-server pattern (*Figure 2.2*) appeared from the need for a server to work with several clients that want to access the same service.

This pattern has two sides, as expressed by the name: the client or clients and the server that serves the clients. The workflow is very straightforward: the client requests or modifies some data through some service or APIs, and the server responds as expected. It is not mandatory to have both the client and the server in the same place; they can communicate while being on different servers. In this case, the client is the one that initiates the communication while the server stays open to these requests.

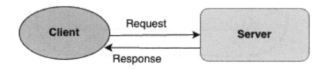

Figure 2.2 – The basic structure of the client-server pattern

The flow is easy to work with, as the client is the one that initiates the communication, and the data is easily delivered to the client. This results in good performance and low maintenance in the product's life cycle.

Downsides

A point to give extra attention to here is security. Ensure you control any input from the client and the way that data is carried between the client and the server.

At the same time, the server can become a performance bottleneck and a single point of failure.

The Model-View-Controller pattern

When I started working with the **Model-View-Controller** (**MVC**) pattern, I sometimes found it hard to understand where the line between the components was drawn. Later, I discovered that it is one of those patterns that lets you work simultaneously in different areas (logic, user interface, and data management, for example) of the application.

Simply put, the MVC pattern divides an application into three components: model, view, and controller (*Figure 2.3*):

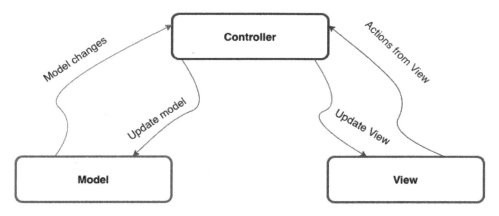

Figure 2.3 – The MVC pattern structure

Each component or layer of the MVC structure has a different role:

- Model – This is the layer where the core functionality and data logic reside. This is where we handle data logic and the interaction with the database. Please note that it does not contain logic that shapes how the data is presented to the final user in the UI – that is the controller's job.

- View – The UI displays the information and ways to interact with the user. In this layer, we handle data presentation and dynamically render the results to the user.

- Controller – This manages the requests from the user and interacts with the model and the view as a consequence of delegating the type of info they need. The controller can be seen as an entry point into the application. A controller might interact with many different models (in the model layer) and views (in the view layer).

By using this pattern correctly, we can quickly build a decoupled system that allows us to reuse code and facilitates the organization of the code base.

Downsides

Because it seems straightforward at first sight, it can immediately be considered as an option for simple applications without considering the complexity that it brings when it is not really understood.

The microservices pattern

For the longest time, we worked with monoliths and tried to work around their complexity. As applications developed and became bigger and bigger, so did the monolith, becoming harder to extend, maintain, and deploy. Above all, we must consider resource management, which has become an essential concern in today's cloud environments.

While trying different approaches, one successful solution is splitting the monolith into microservices. This way, we decouple services as they become easier to scale, change, and deploy. Another advantage is the possibility of having different teams work on different microservices using different languages (for example, C#, Java, and .NET).

As with any good tool used in the wrong context, we can bring too much complexity. If we don't have the expertise and experience to decouple services completely, we might end up with something worse than a monolith.

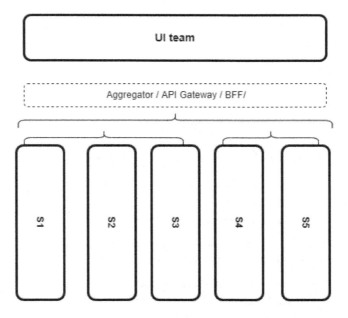

Figure 2.4 – An example structure of the microservices pattern with a middle layer

The microservices architecture gathers several patterns: the branching pattern, the aggregator pattern, the chain-of-responsibility pattern, and the API gateway design pattern are just a few. The goal is to provide a method for managing data to create a service that can be quickly and independently consumed.

Microservices architecture has become very popular because of the benefits that it brings. Still, as with any good tool, if you use it without reading the instructions, you risk breaking it. So, let's cover the principles of good microservice architecture:

- Scalability

- Availability

- Resiliency

- Independent and autonomous

- Decentralized governance

- Failure isolation

- Auto-provisioning

- Continuous delivery through DevOps

Downsides

In real-life applications, sooner or later, although independently designed and built, microservices end up depending on each other in certain areas. Be careful of how you handle these situations and create a sound monitoring plan and fallback in case of failure.

Lastly, I would like to add, not as a downside but more as something to take into consideration when working with distributed teams, that you must consider how you interact with your client and make sure that you provide the service documentation and support for your service to be appropriately consumed without slowing down another team.

The CQRS pattern

If you have ever worked with GraphQL, the **Command and Query Responsibility Segregation** (**CQRS**) pattern will sound familiar. The CQRS pattern (*Fig. 2.5*) focuses on separating two types of operations on data: reading and writing. How does it do this? It does so with the help of two big entities:

- Queries – They are responsible for getting the data that will be displayed in the UI from the database. Their role is only to retrieve the data and they have no way of changing anything.

- Commands – They are responsible for changing data. Compared to queries, which only execute a single operation, commands can carry out a wide range of actions, such as **Create, Read, Update, and Delete**. Commands are handled by CommandHandlers that return an event, which can have two states, successful or failed, depending on the status of the command.

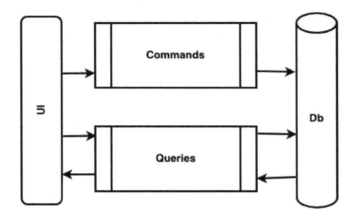

Figure 2.5 – An example structure of a CQRS pattern

One of the advantages of this separation is that in many scenarios and applications, we have more operations that read data than operations that change or delete data. Hence, we gain a lot on the performance side.

The separation between queries and commands brings good performance, as queries usually return a more significant amount of data than commands that modify data, and are easier to manage.

Downsides

I've been in teams where CQRS was the first option, but the lack of deeper understanding at some point added a lot of complexity to the code base, resulting in anything but a CQRS implementation. Working with this pattern requires a certain level of experience and overview. Why? Because you might be bringing a lot of complexity and duplication to a simple **Create, Read, Update, and Delete (CRUD)** application that could work better with less sophisticated architectural patterns.

UI patterns

An area that has evolved significantly in recent years is the UI. Where we previously handled simple operations involving HTML, CSS, and some JavaScript, now we must also concern ourselves with maintainability, testability, state management, and performance. This is precisely why the client evolved as an essential and independent side of the application and explains why the need for patterns that resolve more specific UI-related problems was inevitable. We will discuss some of the most popular patterns and approaches in this section.

Before going into each UI pattern, I would like to underline some concepts that we will mention in some of the following sections, primarily dynamic and static websites.

In a static site, we have one or more HTML files on the server. When the user enters a specific web page, these files are served to the user by the server. Everything is pre-rendered. These websites are a good choice for personal blogs, presentation business sites, or other types that don't need any dynamic section but need search engine optimization.

On the other hand, dynamic sites display different types of content depending on the user that opens it, the time of the day, or data changes. Dynamic web pages are generated in real time based on user data.

Micro frontends

The micro-frontends approach extends the idea of microservices to the client as straightforwardly as that. The UI layer developed alongside the needs of users and the evolution of technology. As a result, it is hard to maintain or even build a single team. That's why we needed a new approach, a way to split the frontend monolith and make it easier to develop, extend, and maintain for different teams.

Migrating from a monolith to micro frontends starts with thinking of features as different pieces that compose a web application. Each feature is owned by a diverse team that puts its total effort into and focuses on a single element of the business.

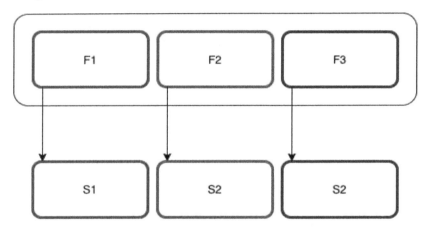

Figure 2.6 – The simple structure of a micro-frontends architecture

One of the best results of micro frontends is that we can split into independent smaller teams and deliver more intentionally and, in many cases, more quickly. As teams can work independently, they have more time to understand and develop their part of the whole. Besides the ownership and business understanding, we will also have a more manageable code base. Consequently, we can build and deploy independent apps that don't share runtimes or states.

Modularity also brings many benefits to testing. It becomes easier to control and test more minor separate features.

While using micro frontends, you don't have to worry about only using one technology. Micro frontends are technology agnostic, meaning every team can work with a different tech stack. Just be careful how you integrate and manage shared areas.

Downsides

Suppose we discussed the benefits of modularity in the context of isolated testing when we discussed whole app testing. In that case, things get a bit complicated, and we can easily lose the bigger picture. Make sure you consider end-to-end testing in the beginning and create a plan for measuring quality.

Another disadvantage is that we might become a bit too focused as a team on our specific features and find it hard to align later as we extend the product in multiple directions. Although we work in different teams, we are still building the same product. An overview of quality attributes, alignment on best practices and principles, and basic knowledge about DevOps should not be absent. Create team sync meetings to keep everyone on the same page and ensure that the product is quality-oriented.

Jamstack

Jamstack is an architectural pattern that allows developers to work with a static website in terms of performance, scalability, and security. Mathias Biilmann, who came up with this name, describes it as a modern web development architecture based on client-side JavaScript, reusable APIs, and prebuilt markup. The core idea is to create a decoupled architecture by splitting the JavaScript code, the APIs, and the markup between the client and server. Jamstack promises to be faster, cheaper, and more secure than the traditional client-server approach, whereas, in *Figure 2.7*, the application is being served dynamically from the server:

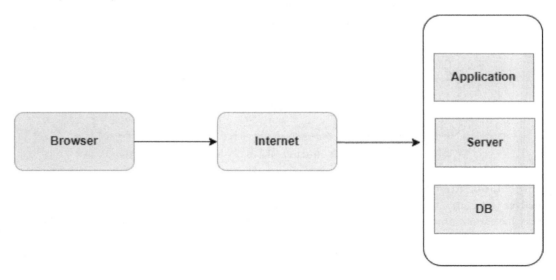

Figure 2.7 – The client-server approach

Jamstack, on the other hand, has no traditional backend server. In Jamstack, once the browser has loaded the static site, you can generate HTTP requests, using JavaScript's help, to third-party services – database and identity management, for example (*Figure 2.8*):

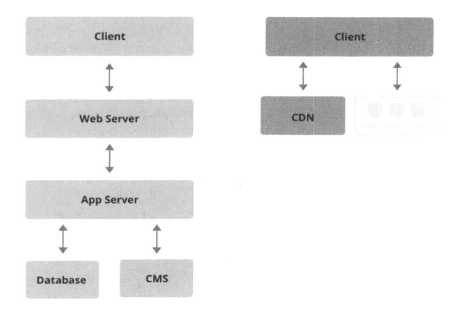

Figure 2.8 – A Jamstack structure (source: https://jamstack.org/)

As our browsers run on JavaScript, it is the right tool for creating a great user experience. Eliminating a web server and using a CDN brings the most benefits because, for example, the CDN does not process requests and just serves files, so the requests are faster. Add to this the fact that CDNs can serve on a network closer to the user than a traditional server, which minimizes latency.

This, at the same time, is mandatory. If you want to use another language, that is fine. You have the flexibility to choose the proper library or framework for the job.

Jamstack promises two principles: decoupling and pre-rendering. The entire client is prebuilt into highly optimized static pages and assets during the build process by performing pre-rendering. On the other hand, it promises the creation of a clean separation between services and systems by decoupling the assistance needed. As a result, each component becomes easier to upgrade, extend, and maintain. One of the best cases where Jamstack works at its finest is in the case of web portals, personal blogs, or e-commerce sites.

Downsides

Dynamic environments are not a good fit for Jamstack. If you want to build more than static pages and need plugins, you will have to put in some extra effort or make manual changes since many related features are not available by default.

Flux

Flux is an architectural pattern for frontend development introduced by Facebook for building single-page applications. This pattern arose from the need to improve scalability and performance on the client side, mainly in state management. With the fast development of frontend operations, it became complicated to manage communication between components, primarily when they were not directly related. Initially, it was thought of as a way to organize flows in React, but the pattern was slowly approached in various scenarios and applications that use other technologies.

The Flux pattern uses a unidirectional data flow to manage data from different and unrelated parts of the application. The approach that the Flux pattern brings consists of organizing flows in the application using the following structures and steps (*Fig. 2.9*):

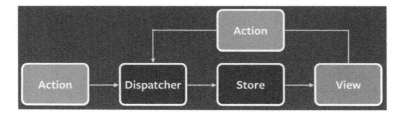

Figure 2.9 – The flux pattern structure (source: `https://facebook.` `github.io/flux/docs/in-depth-overview`)

Let's look at some important steps that flux works with and how the link to each other to create the pattern's flow as we use it in so many applications nowadays:

- Store – The store is where the state is managed and organized. The state can be any value from the data in the database or a Boolean representing the state of a toggle in the UI. The store, however, is more complex, as it gathers all the states that need to be worked with and managed through a specific API. The store has events for listening and emitting changes depending on the state's status. The only way to perform a state change is by passing the action to the dispatcher.

- Dispatcher – This is a way to dispatch a specific action to the store to perform the corresponding changes on a piece of state (for example, to request data from the API).

- Views – Views are represented by the components that trigger a certain action on the state due to user interaction. Views subscribe to the changes happening in the part of the store that they use and rerender.

- Actions – Actions are objects that contain information that distinguishes different types of changes in the state. Actions can come both from the view as the result of user interaction and some parts of code logic (different actions can trigger the retrieval of data from the API and determine the selection of an item).

- Action creators – These are basically represented by functions that create and dispatch actions.

Let's take a regular flow as an example to understand how all these structures work together. I click a button from the view and the view dispatches an action to the store where my piece of state is placed. The state is modified or not depending on the kind of action I have triggered. After the store changes, the view listens to it and rerenders accordingly with the new data. Keep in mind that the flow is unidirectional.

Downsides

Used in the wrong context, the flux pattern can bring a lot of unnecessary complexity. If our application is small or doesn't need serious state management, we can try other ways to improve communication between components, such as services or parent-child communication. Assess your context thoroughly before using this kind of approach.

Summary

An architectural pattern is a solution to a recurring problem that we encounter along the way in different contexts. By researching, we can start to build our architecture using an existing pattern and then see how we can extend it to check quality attributes and satisfy our requirements.

The need for architectural patterns concerning specific application areas became inevitable once the needs of users evolved and new, more performant tools took over the market. This is how we started working with UI patterns.

The next chapter will destroy some myths about architecture and architects.

3
Myths about Architecture

For a long time, we had to deal with the idea that the development team members should keep their attention on coding and not bother with architectural concepts since those are not their concern. This is such a wrong way of looking at things. There are so many benefits to having at least an overview of the architectural vision of what you are working on. For me, the switch happened at a moment when I felt stuck and didn't understand what I was building and how that feature would fit into the architectural picture. The moment I stepped away from the IDE, I started to understand better what I was building and came up with better solutions instead of complaining about the same problems I couldn't understand. Working toward consistency in the implemented processes, features to code, and best practices, I could see where some technical guidance might be needed. I was able to visualize components' interactions from a higher level. It changed my perspective on my daily work.

In time, I gained confidence in questioning everything. Rules I followed for a long time now had a big question mark above them. This is how I came to dispel some myths I encountered along the way in my years of working in software development.

In this chapter, we will go over some of the many myths that we encounter in our careers as developers. We will destroy these myths one by one and discuss some approaches to handling some difficult situations.

We'll debunk the following myths in this chapter:

- Architecture never changes
- Only the architect cares about architecture
- Architecture is not about coding

Myth no.1: Architecture never changes

Users' needs evolve, the market is changing, competition is tough, technologies evolve and change, and teams' structures and compositions also vary. On one side, we are lucky to be working in such a dynamic environment where technical evolution happens constantly. Technological evolution and ever-changing user and business requirements keep us in the loop, always giving us the satisfaction of learning something new. We grow as professionals and learn new approaches and technologies. This can become a "learning haven." The real challenge comes when we have to make decisions that depend on our knowledge. This includes weighing why one technology is better than the other, what risks certain decisions bring, and what the costs of some requested changes are. The challenge is building products that meet our stakeholders' needs today and are open to evolution for future requests. To make informed decisions, we need to develop skills and experience that we can use later as architects.

There is a misconception that the architect has to be the best developer in the team, but we must understand that mastering the whole stack is almost impossible. That would be massive pressure on one person because owning every detail, framework, and library is impracticable, considering the speed at which the tech stack evolves. There is something more valuable than running through technologies and trying to cover them. That is the ability to switch between implementation details and the big architectural picture.

Predicting the future is hard

We previously discussed the quality of being able to predict and adapt to change. Making decisions concerning architectural aspects is a key aspect that we must discuss and understand because those decisions have a huge impact. One good practice in software development is to avoid making decisions until the very last moment because there is a high level of uncertainty, especially in architecture. Why is that? Some things are hard to predict because the tech stack and the client needs are ever-changing. Any fixed decision might take us on the wrong path.

Changes can be from both technical and business perspectives. As technologies and tools evolve or change, our stakeholders can change their views, and in order to create the best product, we have to accept that. Also, at any point in time, while gaining experience and more control in product evolution, we might want to change some characteristics or improve some. We are aware of this, and trying to delay the moment of making a decision as much as possible is equally essential to building a system with the capacity to be changed and extended. But we can't delay the moment of deciding architectural matters forever. We have to decide on something with the information we have eventually.

Another good strategy is gathering feedback and perspectives from all stakeholders, not getting lost in the details, and accepting that creating an architecture that will also fit future requirements is more important than creating the perfect architecture for the current conditions. Ultimately, our software has to be prepared for these scenarios and allow changes to be made step by step and in iterations.

Let's look at some constructive attitudes that can differentiate a good architect from a bad one:

- **Iteratively analyze and update architecture.**

  Architecture is not something discussed in the beginning and then forgotten somewhere in the attic. Architecture changes, so we must integrate technology and business requirements correctly. In the decision-making process, there is a strong need for awareness of the state of architecture and its implementation.

- **Keep up with the tech stack.**

  We are users; we know how our needs, expectations, and standards of what is a good product evolve. All these products that passed the test of time and are still leading in the market did so because they had the ability to change and embrace the technical stack evolution. We also need to take care of this ability in our products. Continually evaluate the changes in the tech stack and see how a particular tool might integrate into your context to bring benefits. Don't get lost in promises, however. These days, even the technical context has become a victim of marketing, so try to look at the inner workings of the frameworks and libraries and see whether they bring advantages to your application.

- **Architect in terms of problems and solutions.**

  There is no perfect, complete, and fits-all-cases architecture. Many approaches have shown, over time and in different scenarios, that they can be successful. But achieving success in the same way for your product comes down to two questions:

  - What is the problem you want to solve?

  - How is your product going to evolve?

  The first question helps us make a good choice in terms of the structure we want to use. The second one, since we discussed that building architecture is a road full of obstacles, makes us think about choosing an approach where we have a more negligible cost of change in the future. This kind of mindset pushes us to build evolvable structures.

- **Keep it simple.**

  An idea that I've always believed in is: don't overthink; always keep it simple. Build step by step while keeping in mind best practices and changes in your context. Steve Jobs said in one of his popular speeches: "*You can't connect the dots looking forward; you can only connect them looking backward. So you have to trust that the dots will somehow connect in your future.*" Don't strive to create the greatest architectural approach, but try to build a strong product at any point in time. Later, you will see that you created the best architecture by constantly focusing on quality attributes and stakeholders' requirements.

- **Think like a stakeholder.**

  When you have to make an architectural decision and feel the pressure of making the best decision, take a deep breath and think about this: "The expectation from me is not to create something that team members will blindly follow and that will fit every future need and scenario. The goal is actually to consider making architectural decisions or even build a system's architecture as an ongoing process, and this process, to give the best results, needs to be transparent for all the stakeholders." Then, get together and work on understanding what your stakeholders want and need. How do we do this? First, by understanding who is the stakeholder. Generally speaking, stakeholders come in three categories:

- The ones that develop and work for the product

- The ones that use the product

- The ones that, even though they are not using the product or developing it, are still facilitating some processes that help the product

The development team will always be the closest to and most involved in the product. They are the ones that have to switch places with users constantly. A popular way of doing things is to ask from time to time: "As a user, would I like this or that?" As a developer, an architect, or part of the development team, you must always be aware of the product's direction and ensure that every business person understands the technical implications of every change.

Sometimes users know that they want a certain kind of feature. Still, they don't understand the technical implications or whether it is integrated correctly into the user flow. Actually, in many cases, users realize it is not what they wanted after seeing a feature they requested in the application. As humans, we look for a certain feeling and ease that a functionality provides and think that the way we see that functionality in another flow will also work well in our product, but the truth is, this is not always the case. It's essential to explain the costs of every requirement, explain the implications, negotiate, and come up with suggestions.

You can have the best technologies, the best-quality gates, and quality attributes, but if no one uses your application, all the effort is in vain. One important quality of every organization is the ability to be agile and adapt to change and stakeholders' needs along the way. Of course, the technical choices are still important, but they shouldn't run the show but rather be a way of facilitating the process of meeting customer needs.

Myth no.2: Only the architect cares about architecture

I believe that making coding a part of your role as an architect is a game-changer. I've worked in teams where the architect opened the IDE and started coding, and I've worked in groups where the architect was only a title; I almost had no idea who that was, and I met them only when I was building a feature that impacted the architecture. From my experience, an architect that stays close to the team becomes naturally more engaged with the team and, as a result, understands the impact of the architectural decisions and the reality of the existing code base that tries to fit those decisions. I was lucky enough to be part of a team where the development team was consulted regarding some necessary architectural changes. The architect wanted to validate his architectural perspective in real-life scenarios and with people who would implement his vision in the end. At the same time, by having this kind of team discussion, the developers got the chance to understand how those decisions are being made, the high-level implications and risks, and how higher-level structures interact. It created the feeling that we were building something extraordinary, and we were. For the second example, unfortunately, the result was a confused and frustrated team because many issues surfaced when different components were integrated. I'm not saying that the architect should take tasks from the board, but they should be an integral part of the team.

I think that this kind of collaboration and feedback process in the team brings benefits to two significant areas:

- The architect will better understand the context of the application, components, and code base from a developer's perspective and make more informed and realistic decisions.

- The team will understand the impact and importance of their work and trust the architect more.

I want to make a disclaimer regarding whether, in having a collaborative team, the role of an architect is still relevant. The question in this situation is whether we still need an architect or whether the team can self-organize. We have to keep it accurate. Having a self-organizing team is something to strive for, but in reality, it is hard to achieve. Team composition can easily change, the level of engagement is different from one team member to the other, and in the end, we always need someone to keep us on track, no matter how engaged we are with the product we are building. However, if the product is stable, has no impactful changes, and the team is organized and has a high level of experience, the continuous presence of an architect is not mandatory. Previously, I discussed a general situation with an evolving product, a complex structure, many stakeholders, big teams, and so on.

So, can any developer be an architect? Developers can grow, with the emphasis on *grow*, into becoming an architect. This is why we need to understand two things:

- Having an overview and occasional engagement with a system's architecture does not make you an architect.

- The fact that you have an architect does not make you free of the responsibility of how the system evolves or the quality of the project.

As a developer, you might be undertaking parts of the software architecture role without keeping in mind that there is a big difference between contributing to the architecture and being responsible for it.

As already discussed, the architecture is a blueprint defining high-level units of our system and how they interact and evolve in relationship with one another. Choosing the right or wrong architectural pattern will determine how scalable, reliable, performant, and secure the system will be. On the other hand, a system design shapes things more at the code level, such as how each component works and the purpose of each element.

A solid system design helps the development team be more efficient and organized in terms of understanding its responsibilities of functions, modules, and classes and what they can or can't do. This can be done by identifying a system's design so we can later decide what design patterns we should use in specific contexts.

Extending this a bit, in a discussion about design and architecture, Grady Booch nicely talks about how "architecture represents the significant design decisions that shape a system, where significance is measured by the cost of change." Significant decisions are architecture, and the rest is design. Later on, in *Chapter 7, Leveraging Soft Skills*, we will look a bit deeper at the subject of decision making, but before that, to conclude: software architecture is focused on the entire system, while software design focuses on a more specific level.

Simon Brown nicely expresses architectural decisions as ones you cannot reverse without much effort; you can't change an architectural decision in an afternoon.

Because we can't change an architectural decision in an afternoon, the first step in architecting software is understanding what is significant and why. When talking about substantial matters, we talk about concepts such as the technologies chosen to work with or the high-level structure and understanding of how to tackle risks. Understanding these matters makes a difference to our development team.

It's easy to think that if you are writing good code and following some well-tested approaches, knowledge about architecture is neglectable. There are some benefits of getting an overview of what we are building. From understanding how components in the system should interact to component responsibility and the cost of what components I am changing or creating when developing a feature, it is imperative to have at least a slight understanding of the architecture I am working on.

This myth is strongly related to the next one, as it focuses on how architecture is connected to more than just the high-level components. As we will see in the next section, architecture has much to do with coding.

Myth no.3: Architecture is not about coding

From what we've discussed, maybe with some exceptions, architecture is a part of the development process, the part that is later taken over and implemented by the team. Architecture is not about forgetting about implementation details and getting drowned in abstractions but about keeping them balanced. I think we become good architects when moving carefully from one to the other.

Software architecture is all about understanding how the system works as a whole. Going from contributing to the architecture to being responsible and making decisions to grow a product is a process. The first step of this process is being honest with our experience level and what areas we need to focus on to proceed to the next level as professionals.

We need to be aware of the differences that help us to evolve. For example, as a programmer, your constant focus is on details, while architects focus most of their time on the whole picture, and most of the time, architects make decisions that programmers have to live with. There is always context to change the perspective and evolve from your level. Take any learning opportunity and make it a cornerstone of your career.

As an architect, you can better understand the context of the application, components, and code base from a developer's perspective and make more informed, realistic decisions.

Of course, when we discuss the role with a high level of involvement in many areas, it is hard to stay and code. The reality is that, yes, sometimes an architect might bring more value by having a focus on high-level discussions and abstract architectural structures than coding, but there are many methods that we can use to keep in touch with the code base and check the team's technical level and way of working, such as the following:

- Switch roles – collaboration
- Pair programming
- Pull request (PR) reviews
- Architecture unit tests
- DevOps quality gates

Let's look at all of these methods in detail.

Switch roles – collaboration

Yes, as an architect, you should bring your own best practices, approaches, overviews on design, and patterns that add more value to some technologies or help you choose the right one in the project context. But when it comes to keeping an eye on details, such as low-level code, I think it is true that value exists in using the technical expertise of the team. The role of a software architect can sometimes be that of another team member when contributing to an idea. We must create a trustful and collaborative environment where people can express their ideas and expertise.

Pair programming

Pair programming is one of the best ways to learn, gain confidence in your work, get instant feedback, and create trust within the team. Usually, we have two developers (one who writes code and the other who contributes and gives feedback), and then they change roles. This approach works very nicely and brings many benefits when we have new members within the team or different levels of experience between team members. But this can also be a lovely way for developers to learn from the architect and vice versa. The architect can also use this exact technique to keep track of the commitment and architectural understanding of the team and check whether the team can meet delivery deadlines. Also, by doing code reviews with the development team, you can get feedback on the architecture while helping the team understand areas you detect were unclear.

PR reviews

Another approach to keep track of how things are evolving at the code level and how the development team stays aligned with the architectural view is to do a PR review from time to time. We are human; we are prone to error even when we are extra careful, which is why it's good to have some automatic steps that check best practices in our code. It is also of great help to have another colleague evaluate our code. From time to time, this colleague can be the architect. This way, the architect can keep close to the team, gain their trust, and give feedback. In return, the architect gets input from the team on how they implement the architecture. Above all, from the leadership perspective, the process we've discussed helps both the architect and developer grow as professionals.

Architecture unit tests

If we are talking about a team with different levels of experience, sometimes it is hard to keep track of understanding each architectural pattern as an architect. A way of making sure that we don't miss architectural details or introduce some unwanted dependencies is by creating some architectural unit tests. Some libraries and frameworks facilitate this (such as ArchUnit or out-of-the-box tools for checking the structure as we have in mono repo). This way, the team has automatic feedback and can immediately fix missed things.

Another way to have instant feedback on what we are building but still check on the code we write is using **test-driven development** (**TDD**). TDD is a software development approach in which we first define and create the tests that will check our code and then write the code, step by step, repeating the process until the functionality is done. We generate test cases for each functionality, write the test, and when the test fails, we can write code that will help the test pass. As a result, we will avoid creating bugs by leaving untested areas or changing existing ones in the code. We will have a simple and easy-to-test code base because small methods and structures are easier to test. It is like a healthy life cycle if you don't over-engineer and get lost in abstractions, so keep it simple.

DevOps quality gates

Having strong quality gates helps you review your work, examine how changes impact existing functionality, and use metrics that allow you to track how you meet specific quality attributes. At each stage, you can define a particular set of metrics, and if they are complete, you can move on to the next until you've ensured that you're delivering a stable version to production. If any of the metrics are not met, you can detect the error early enough, which will have a low impact, and fix the issue before it gets to your users.

Architecture is also about coding because all the decisions we make as architects impact what the team will work on. At the same time, we make more informed and reality-oriented decisions by having awareness and feedback from the group.

Summary

In this chapter, we learned that architecture is not something that is fixed once and lasts forever. The ever-changing market, competition, technologies, and trends require us to rethink our product to meet the needs of stakeholders. To do this and deliver a strong effect, we use the technologies that integrate best with those needs.

We also learned that the process of shaping the architecture and the development process are not concepts that work against each other. Understanding the architectural strategies and why certain decisions were made in a certain way helps developers be more engaged with their work, come up with solutions, and contribute. On the other hand, architects can get feedback directly from the team on how architectural decisions are implemented in reality.

In the next chapter, we will look more closely at some quality attributes that can help us create robust systems.

4
Discussing What Good Architecture Is

We have been discussing decisions, architectural patterns, and approaches to creating good architecture, but the question now arises: What exactly is good architecture?

From the start, I have to say that there is no failure-proof definition on the way. I don't believe in the perfect blueprint. I think architecture evolves, so much that it needs great attention and enough knowledge to be shaped as strongly as possible. I must repeat what I said in the previous chapter: any of the discussed patterns can fail if used in the wrong context, no matter how good they are.

Generally, in the discussions or workshops that I've been a part of, when the question about what makes a good architecture came up, most of the time, some keywords were repeated, most commonly *performance*, *security*, *scalability*, *reliability*, and then, as the discussion evolved, many others would be discussed (see *Figure 4.1*):

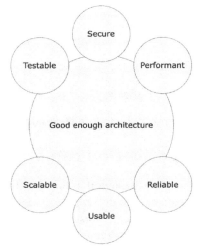

Figure 4.1 – Some characteristics of a "good enough" architecture

But when we discuss what good architecture is, the right approach is not to think about the best architectural perspective that you have ever seen and its characteristics but to look at what you know about your system (the one that you have to build), what other information you need, and what the best architecture that you can shape right now with what you have is.

Of course, the architectural plan will give a significant direction of where the system is heading, so we need a solid and stable start. So yes, as I mentioned before, the result that we had in time while keeping an eye on some characteristics (performance, security, scalability, and reliability) show that, in time, they are necessary and worth considering. At the root, we must ensure that having an architectural plan leads us towards building a complete product characterized by scalability, performance, security, and reliability: a system that can be easily tested and used. Ignoring any of these will result in technical debt, team frustration, bugs, and failure, and in time, we will start losing users and have issues at the business level.

Don't forget that architecture is not only about tech stuff; it takes more than just a very well-shaped technical plan to build a good product. It's about human resources, business, marketing, dealing with different stakeholders, costs, decisions, and risks. It's about decisions and the ability to learn from errors.

To ensure that we have a complete overview of architecture evolution, we have to team up with developers, especially at the beginning of developing the product. This way, we ensure that while we are building, we are considering the end goal at each step.

So, again, what is good architecture?

Good architecture takes into consideration at least the following attributes:

- Consider how your application can scale in time
- Provide good performance step by step
- Is your architectural approach reliable?
- Ensure security at all levels
- Create a testable architecture
- How do you know that your app is usable?

We will discuss them in the following sections and understand their impact.

Consider how your application can scale in time

The usage of software products has gone through the roof. Our need to work quickly through our daily tasks has increased, and our patience has decreased just as much. At the same time, the market evolves, and since the competition develops, we must create quality and up-to-date products. This is why we must always be ready to change and extend our architectural direction, starting with the mindset that we need our application always to be prepared to scale.

Ignoring scalability is one of the most dangerous things regarding the application life cycle because the consequences can be disastrous. As we discussed, as architects, we need to understand the direction of the application and what we want to achieve in the best-case scenarios. Not considering scalability will eventually push us to make uninformed decisions since we lack data about the next step and find ourselves needing to consume many resources to change some areas just because we did not consider several possibilities from the start.

Before going too deep into risks, it may be better to start by clearly defining scalability and ensuring we look at it from all perspectives.

Scalability is a system's ability to be ready to handle both big workloads and decreases by keeping the costs directly proportional as much as possible.

When we think about software systems, we often consider costs related to software tools or infrastructure, but scalability is influenced by more than this. When we talk about system scaling, we talk about software, infrastructure, developers, deployment, business people, and testing.

I want to stop for a second and discuss testing as it is challenging, especially since many of the scalable metrics are available in production environments, making it hard to reproduce in the development environment, at least not without increased effort. Therefore, create a custom strategy for handling scalability. Equally impacted, or even more, is deployment as the cost of deployment rises significantly.

Along the way, two approaches have evolved in terms of scalability: vertical and horizontal.

Horizontal versus vertical scalability

Vertical scalability means investing in robust and more extensive hardware that complies with the upgraded requirements. Your resources will be handled with more hardware power. The problem with this is the investment, as it can become costly. The problem with this is that there is a limit to what "big" hardware means; therefore, another approach has appeared – horizontal scalability. Instead of adding more extensive hardware, add more copies of the same hardware you already have.

We can't talk about and work toward scalability without considering best practices.

For example, a system composed of loosely coupled components is easier to modify because your changes are isolated, and it is easier to control side effects. A loosely coupled system is easier to work with when considered from a scalability perspective. You can work with each component, considering their particular needs for scalability, and consider splitting responsibility between different teams.

Another point worth mentioning is state management. A stateless system is way easier to scale but is not very useful. You can't do much with it. There is no attraction to using a stateless app with all the features and possibilities that users expect. So, what do we do to ensure that our system will stay consistent and clean when discussing state management? Isolate. Depending on the architectural pattern you use, you can extract the state in a data layer or organize it in a way that allows you to keep it as independent as possible.

Everything that we've discussed revolves a lot around predicting the future. Although not easy, we can prepare for challenges and changes. At the same time, if you have been working on a product for several years, overthinking, in the beginning, might make you invest time in functionalities you will never need. So, this is a tricky road to walk. This is why it is good to build incrementally, step by step, even if you fail to repair just as fast. Overthinking is not OK, and rushing is risky, but you can't just stay in one place. You need to experiment, try, fail, and rewind until you find the recipe that works well for your context.

Here are some other characteristics that we will discuss in this chapter that are strongly related to scalability:

- **Performance**: Our application should stay performant no matter how many more users or operations it gains. The user should not notice that your application has scaled.

- **Availability**: This is a straightforward one. Your system should always be available. If there is any need for updates, try to do it when the user usage is as small as possible to avoid high impact.

- **Reliability** is the ability of your system to work without failure for an extended period, independent of how this evolves or scales.

Just as we were discussing in the previous chapters, architecture changes evolve together with requirements and the market, and at the same time, scalability requirements do too. Don't panic; keep an open mind, research, build in terms of evolvable structures, and fix bad decisions on the go.

Provide good performance step by step

We cannot discuss good architecture without touching on the subject of performance. As systems become more complex and users have more demands than ever, the number of operations and transactions increases significantly.

Performance is about doing some operations in an expected time using the available resources. We can control performance on one side by ensuring resources are well managed and adapting as the application scales. You will know if you have lousy performance, and your users will know too because awful performance impacts usability.

Even the most complex and popular applications have performance issues related to response time.

When we consider performance matters, we can't ignore other quality attributes. Performance is strongly related to scalability, usability, and reliability. Inadequate management or overlooking one can impact all of the others.

Besides resource management, we can look at architecture from another perspective: code-wise. Many times, we have performance issues even before scaling or using many resources, so there are some checks that I consider important and that can be done in the development phase:

- Check complexity
- Check queries
- Ensure modularity
- Clear business logic from the UI
- Identify a chatty UI
- Identify big and unnecessary payloads
- Check coupling and cohesion
- Evaluate how compliant are you to your architectural view

Let's understand these points in detail:

- **Complexity** is something that we sometimes overlook. When rushing to complete the task at hand, we use the first solution that does the job. It might not seem impactful at a method or class level, but complexity adds up at the application level. When we look for complexity in our code we check from certain operations' time complexity to class dependencies.

- As the application and operations get more complex, we might have to work at the database level with **complex queries**. Make sure you check them for performance and use best practices.

- **Modularity** measures how components of your system can be used independently of the context they have been created in and how reusable they can get. Modularity helps us think about reusable structures, significant performance improvements, and how big the code base gets. A modular system is easier to maintain, test, and extend.

- Another way to look at performance is how complex your **UI operations** are. Doing specific procedures can be more expensive on the UI than on the server side.

- As in the code base, it is essential to keep dependencies as clean as possible regarding architectural components. It is essential to have **high cohesion** and **low coupling**. These principles go well with the previous one. High maintenance and reusability are achieved by keeping the system as clean and modular as possible.

- **Chattiness** is achieved when instead of evaluating existing API strategies and maybe redesigning some areas, we keep adding new APIs for each requirement from the client. This way, we send complex adapter operations to the client and have a big load over the network, which will give us headaches regarding latency and performance.

- On the other side, while avoiding calling too many APIs, we tend to add the properties needed to existing ones. This leads us to have an enormous payload to travel over the network, resulting in a slow response time.

- Last but not least, a way of measuring architectural performance is with the help of tools and metrics such as static code analysis tools (for example, SonarQube) or tools that provide you with a dependency graph and some customizable rules, depending on the architectural approach we chose (some monorepo tools, as nx, provide this kind of feature).

Is your architectural approach reliable?

A reliable system is a system that functions as expected in certain conditions, for a certain period, and in predefined environments. Although it is a characteristic challenged by customer context, reliability does not depend on design or flows but on how often and in what ways does the system fail continuously. As discussed in the previous chapters, predicting change and product evolution is crucial. In addition, the idea of measuring reliability can take quality to the next level.

If you think stakeholders might change their perspectives dramatically, there is still room for discussion, and you need more answers about what they need, not just what they want. Or if you fear that trends might push you to change the technology you use, maybe you are not that sure about your choice, and you need to research more on this and look for a more suitable technology. The technologies you use are some of the most complex decisions to change later in a product's life, so you want to be confident with your decision when you start.

The list of factors, of which we can only see a small example in *Figure 4.2*, can go on and on, but what we need to keep in mind is that even from the start, the need for change is going to appear, and we will need to prioritize and create a risk management plan to tackle whatever we know might happen:

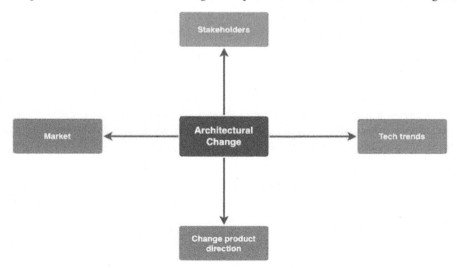

Figure 4.2 – Factors that influence change in a system

Simply put, a system is reliable when it performs as expected under normal conditions for a scheduled period.

Reliability is hard to define and achieve because it also depends upon usability, performance, maintainability, and other quality metrics in general.

Ensure security at all levels

Security is one of the essential crosscutting concerns for an application as it implies that by using different tools, specifications, processes, and applications, we are protecting an application. It is important to note that security is about protecting, preventing, and mitigating different types of possible threats.

When discussing architecture security, we discuss a set of processed tools and teams working together to achieve threat detection and prevention.

Working on security can impact other quality attributes. For example, actions to support security might reduce performance in some situations and the other way around (see *Figure 4.3*):

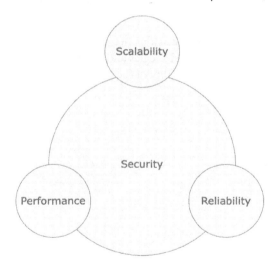

Figure 4.3 – Example of quality attributes that influence how secure a system might be

As architecture is also evolving, there is a need for security checks and evaluations to be done regularly. This way, we can, in time, determine vulnerabilities and do the necessary actions for the security plan.

Development and testing architecture also need special attention. We need people focused on and responsible for this throughout the application's life cycle. From establishing each role to how often we will have audits and keeping track of the security architecture evolution, it is vital to put attention on security matters at every step.

One of the essential and most visible steps in creating a security plan for an application is establishing the process and rule used for the user to interact with the application, mainly when we discuss sensitive sets of data managed by certain people with specific roles.

We will not go into details regarding specific things to ensure security as these depend on the context and security plan. Still, some things are generally valid that we need to think of to create a healthy and secure architecture. Establish levels of users that can access the application and what areas and data sets need special care. We must know what tasks our users will perform and how much they can manage data through the application.

Beyond users and access management, architects need to understand the requirements clearly. This way, we can start a stable security plan and adapt it step by step, just as we do with architecture.

Create a testable architecture

Testability is about how easy a system is to use and how many issues we find during the testing process. From my experience, testability in both forms results from collaboration, taking care of best practices, and having the same vision in the team.

Depending on architectural and design decisions, we determine how easy it will be to use tests as backups. For this, there is a wide range of strategies and approaches to choose from (see *Figure 4.4*), but don't forget that quality is the responsibility of the entire team, not just QA:

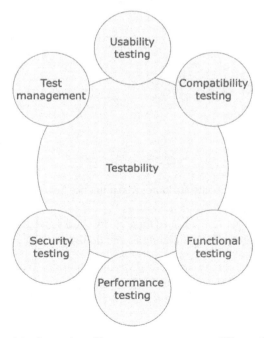

Figure 4.4 – Examples of how to test a system at different levels

When software products are discussed, the general feeling is that we have programmers that develop these fantastic products, and that's that. In reality, one of the essential parts of development is testing. Of course, the discussion can evolve to many ways of testing and in many areas. One of the crucial characteristics to consider when discussing testability is component coupling.

We will not discuss how to test since I consider testability an essential matter that needs a test architect that keeps close with the software architect in terms of vision and good engineering practices.

At some point in the life of our product, we will have to add features we never considered in the beginning. We will have to change some behaviors or rethink entire flows, and we want any change to have as little impact as possible on the other areas. Also, we want to test the changes we are making as soon as possible. Therefore, having a solid testing strategy helps us in development. The level of uncertainty while making changes is smaller since tests back us up. The real value is most visible in the time we save by not having to do a lot of bug fixing, not having to do much debugging, and other manual steps needed in the development process of a quality-oriented product.

Going back a bit to the architectural testing perspective, a point to consider is how isolated components are and how visible the changes going on inside those components are. Try to create features as loosely coupled and pure as possible. This way, you will test and create automated processes that run tests, change, refactor, and optimize.

Remember that, again, you don't want to make the mistake of giving total responsibility for testing to testers. There are tests that developers also create. The testing process may be the most collaborative between developers and testers. When writing code, I expect that this code will be unit tested, end-to-end tested, and so on. Therefore, I try to keep with best practices to make maintaining, extending, rewriting, and testing as smooth and efficient as possible.

When discussing testing, we refer to many stages: unit testing, end-to-end testing, automation, and even architecture. Achieving a high code coverage gives us a high level of stability in the application.

How do you know that your app is usable?

We get the most valuable feedback about whether or not our users can efficiently use our products by measuring usability. We are all users. Some of the applications we use are great, some not so much. We can feel our users' struggle by observing how an application can annoy, slow, or confuse us.

High usability means an excellent user experience for those who use the software system. As a user, I have many applications and products to choose from. Most of the time, the ones that keep me engaged are performant and easy to follow. Increased usability depends on more than the UI. It results from user-oriented design, performance, robust fallback in case of errors, easy-to-follow and remember functionality, and, last but not least, how the user enjoys the whole experience.

As the end users are the most critical stakeholders, we should build a system that helps them achieve their goals by keeping track of the usability of the user experience that we provide. Don't mistake usability with delivering a big load of features that are the latest in user experience. Usability is achieved when all requirements are met, down to the smallest details.

Creating a usable system strongly correlates with user experience because it is strongly related to the users' feelings while using our application. We need to ensure that users want to use our application again and that with each visit, it gets more familiar and easier to follow.

Another vital aspect to consider while thinking about usability is what fallbacks we have in case of errors. Depending on different factors, our applications can sometimes have difficulties that we might not have thought of; as in life, the problem is not that we sometimes have to improve some areas but how we plan on giving users an experience that is as smooth as possible.

A simple way of measuring the system's usability is by asking questions such as: Can users do the actions they expect to do? Are users able to do their tasks quickly? Do users enjoy using the application and use it frequently?

Good feedback on how usable your application is if there is a need to create a guide on using it. If you need to write documentation explaining how the application should be used, or if your users can't find the way to achieve their goals and are always seeking guidance, you might reconsider its usability. Creating this kind of easiness of use and familiarity for our users means that we have to know our users and their context very well: what distractions do they have, what are the most used applications, how often do they use applications, do they use either mobile or desktop more frequently, and so on.

This does not mean we must strive to build an application that meets everyone's ideas or wants. Usability, in the end, is about making some processes more manageable and efficient. This does not mean that we build simple applications. Users need, in the end, efficiency followed by satisfaction while using the products we work on.

In close relationship with usability, we have accessibility and inclusion, and they all together ensure that all our users, without discrimination, have a satisfying user experience. Accessibility provides ways for people with disabilities to interact with our application.

Inclusion comes more on the diversity side. Users should interact efficiently with your product regardless of education, economics, language, culture, and so on.

When discussing usability, we put the user in the center. It is essential to understand their real needs and not to over-engineer. The best feedback we can get when talking about usability comes from the users, so it is vital to create different and diverse groups of users to test the application in real-life scenarios to ensure that we are not responding to preferences but to needs.

Usability is not about having things look pretty and colorful. It is about effectiveness and efficiency first and then the details. When discussing aesthetics, you can have the perfect product, but no one will open it more than once if it is not usable.

Summary

It is vital to research quality attributes and take care of the most impactful to prepare our system for continuous development and future cases.

Quality attributes can influence each other, so we have to pay great attention and prioritize them from the beginning.

Even when discussing quality attributes, just as in everything related to architecture, we need to think in terms of an evolvable process, step by step, understanding the context as we grow.

In the next chapter, we will discuss how architecture and design differ but help shape a quality-oriented system.

5

Design versus Architecture

"The designer is concerned with what happens when a user presses a button, and the architect is concerned with what happens when ten thousand users press a button."

SCEA for Java™ EE Study Guide by Mark Cade and Humphrey Sheil

As discussed in *Chapter 1, The Role of Architecture*, architecture is a base structure upon which we build step by step, one component after another, creating relationships between them. All of this is being realized while considering the whole picture of a product.

When we talk about architecture, we can't avoid discussing design because architecture is confused with design in many cases. This may be because we tend to define architecture abstractly.

Software architecture is a starting point – a base for the system. The decisions we make concerning architecture must fulfill the business and technical requirements while considering quality attributes such as performance and security. The decisions made regarding software architecture significantly impact how the system evolves and achieves its objectives.

When we discuss architecture, we immediately have to concern ourselves with the experience, expertise, and high-level view of the person responsible for creating it. An architect should grow into preparing for all these challenges and responsibilities. Besides technical skills, an architect must also build soft skills. Therefore, when we discuss architecture, we discuss a complex role, impactful decisions, and extreme responsibility.

As already discussed, the architecture is a blueprint defining the high-level units of our system, including how they interact and evolve concerning one another. Choosing the right or the wrong architectural pattern will determine how scalable, reliable, performant, and secure the system will be. But how about design? The following section will detail design and how it differentiates from architecture.

In this chapter, we will learn about the following main topics:

- What is design?
- Discussing design patterns
- Design principles

What is design?

A system's design shapes things more at the code level – the way each component works, the purpose of each element, and concerns of this kind.

A solid system design helps the development team be more efficient and organized in understanding the responsibilities of functions, modules, and classes and what they can or can't do. All of this is made possible by identifying the design of a system to later decide which design patterns we should use in specific contexts.

Extending the discussion about design and architecture, Grady Booch nicely discusses how architecture represents the significant design decisions that shape a system, where the cost of the changes necessary correspond to the significance of these decisions.

Significant decisions are architecture, and the rest is design. Later on, we will go a bit deeper into the decision-making subject. Still, before we get there, we can summarize that software architecture is focused on the entire system. In contrast, software design focuses on a more specific level (at the component or module level, for example).

As very nicely expressed by Simon Brown, architectural decisions are the ones you cannot reverse without much effort. So, think about this when you make an architectural decision or want to change the system and are unsure about the potential impact. Because we can't change an architectural decision in an afternoon, the first step in architecting software is understanding what is significant and why.

When talking about what is significant, we talk about concepts such as the technologies chosen to work with or the high-level structure and our understanding of how to tackle any risks. Understanding these sorts of concepts makes a difference for our development team. Why? Well, it's easy to think that if you write good code and follow some well-tested approaches, your knowledge of architecture is neglectable. There are some meaningful benefits to getting an overview of what we are building, from understanding how the components in a system should interact, which should have what responsibility, to the cost of whatever we are doing when developing a feature. An overview of the architectural dynamics helps us answer questions of this kind.

We've come a long way in this discussion already, and we can agree that taking software from zero to hero is a complicated process, full of risk, collaboration, and impactful decisions. As software has evolved, so have all the steps we must take within an application's life cycle. This might be one of the reasons why we mistake one for the other and make incorrect decisions.

So, let's dive deeper into the discussion about architecture and design. Another reason why they are so easy to confuse is that both are such critical areas of software development.

After what we've discussed thus far, we can say that software architecture combines technical and business requirements and is translated into a high-level structure that defines the system's main components. When building a system's architecture, we have to understand what kind of pattern will suit our needs best and bring about the most significant advantages.

Architecture is also about quality attributes and gives us the direction to meet the security, performance, reliability, and scalability targets discussed in previous chapters. We can sum up by saying that the architecture relates to the decisions that will impact the whole system's development process, so we have to think about extendable structures too.

Software design focuses more on the code level, how specific modules interact and evolve concerning one another, what kind of role each plays, and how we can reuse particular structures and functions.

So basically, design is about the elements that make up the overall structure and, in the end, help achieve the requirements we have previously mentioned. We are trying to define them separately, but it is essential to understand how much they work together.

In *Chapter 3*, *Myths about Architecture*, we discussed how the development team implements the architecture, and why it is essential for the team to be in touch with the architect. Well, the time has come to close the circle. Software design helps developers to translate the given requirements into code.

To work with design, developers should understand the design patterns and fit scenarios. The following section will focus on design patterns and their role.

Discussing design patterns

What are design patterns and how are they different from architectural practices? They are all patterns, so they are all solutions for recurring problems. Design patterns appeared in the 90s and became popular after the book *Design Patterns: Elements of Reusable Object-Oriented Software* was written by Gamma, Helm, Johnson, and Vlissides, who later became known as the Gang of Four. These developers had experienced many situations in which the same problems would repeatedly appear. Therefore, they thought about how they could be solved and whether there were ways to create repeatable solutions to these problems. The answer was yes, so they wrote this book, which would become a key point of reference within software development. The Gang of Four discussed 23 patterns that they identified while working and solving certain problems with **Object-Oriented Programming (OOP)** principles and strategies in mind.

These patterns were organized into three categories depending on their scope:

- Creational patterns are the ones that provide us with ways of creating system components to achieve the maintainability, reusability, and flexibility of the code. These patterns are Factory, Abstract Factory, Builder, Prototype, and Singleton.

- Structural patterns help orchestrate components into bigger and more complex ones while keeping them loosely coupled and performant. Some examples are Adapter, Bridge, Composite, Decorator, Facade, Flyweight, and Proxy.

- Behavioral patterns take care of the responsibilities and behavior of components and how they relate to one another. In this category, we have Chain of Responsibility, Command, Iterator, Mediator, Memento, Observer, State, Strategy, Template Method, and Visitor.

Awareness of these design patterns will ease developers' daily work. Why? Well, why reinvent the wheel when there is already a perfect wheel that has been tested and identified as something we could use to bring value to our work?

By understanding and using these patterns, we can be sure that there are no hidden scenarios and solve the problems in our code or strategies. At the same time, using design patterns helps us stay aligned code-wise at the team level. Building the product in the same direction will be much easier if all team members understand and employ the same design patterns.

Think of design patterns as a language all developers can use to help them maintain regular practices and solutions in a code base. Last but not least, design patterns train a mindset. The mindset is to look at our code from above, see what problems we might encounter with the current solution, find ways to avoid problems, and ultimately optimize this code. Even if we don't use a particular pattern, understanding the existing design patterns help us think of possible strategies in our code along the same vein.

To sum up, there are five reasons why every developer should understand and use design patterns in their work:

- Shifting perspective from the details to an architecture-wide overview.

- Sticking to best practices and writing clean code.

- Detecting rotten design and avoiding mistakes when making design decisions.

- Avoiding making mistakes and building on given experience by using approaches that have been tested in different scenarios and proven to be effective.

- Building experience and individual learning. Following a healthy pattern of learning and coding, we become better at distinguishing between good and bad code.

In previous chapters, we have discussed rotten design and how to detect it. Let's discuss our design principles and how they support the system's development process, maintainability, and flexibility.

Design principles

Design patterns help us with some of the issues we've discussed regarding making changes, reusability, and maintainability. Using design patterns backed by the experience and different work scenarios of highly experienced forebearers, we can be sure that our code will become more readable, decoupled, and aligned with best practices. From my experience, I can say that design patterns have the power to force us to write clean code.

Let's cover some of the design principles that stand behind design patterns:

- SOLID principles (as discussed in *Chapter 1, The Role of Architecture*)
- Encapsulate what varies
- Favor composition over inheritance
- Loose coupling
- KISS
- YAGNI
- DRY

Let's look at these design principles in detail.

Encapsulate what varies – This principle is one of the most straightforward. It teaches us to identify the areas of our system that vary and separate them from what never changes and can be reused. The Strategy, Observer, Decorator, and Adapter design patterns empower these principles.

Favor composition over inheritance – Most of the time, we start with OOP principles at the beginning of our careers. We tend to use inheritance for component interaction, as it is the most straightforward and familiar concept. Inheritance lets you create the behavior of an element by inheriting it from another. This way, the child component uses part of the parent's behavior. A downside of inheritance is that it can bring rigidity to our code when used repeatedly or poorly implemented.

Composition, on the other hand, involves creating new components by compositing components to create more complex functionality. This way, we achieve loosely coupled components in our system. An excellent example of a design pattern that follows this principle is the Builder pattern.

Loose coupling – We achieve this characteristic in our code when each component has as much dependency and knowledge of the inner workings of other components as possible.

Keep It Simple, Stupid (**KISS**) – This principle states that the best approach is to keep our components as small and straightforward as possible, avoiding unnecessary complexity. This way, we write code that is easier to understand and maintain.

You Ain't Gonna Need It (YAGNI) – This principle reminds us that we should only implement and worry about what we want our code to do right now. Don't overcomplicate the development process by thinking about scenarios that may never, and usually will never, happen.

Don't Repeat Yourself (DRY) – This principle states that if you have to use the same code in more than one place, don't copy-paste it. Create a reusable structure and use that.

Next, we will look at how architecture and design work together.

How do design and architecture work together?

Although treated as two stages in the development process, architecture and design work together. While software architecture focuses on a system's structure and high-level components, software design concentrates on a system's details and implementation. We can consider that design combines the inner workings of components and implementation details, algorithms, and data structures.

The architecture is created in the initial stage of the system's development. Later, as we evolve through the development phase, the design surfaces. Along the way, architecture and design overlap and work together, and as we soon realize over time, developers need to understand both. Sometimes, teams have to make critical technical decisions. By understanding both design and architecture, they can also understand how the design decisions they make will help build the architectural vision in the end.

Grady Booch nicely expresses that "all architecture is design, but not all design is architecture." While architecture ultimately contains and is built based on design decisions, this is not valid and vice versa for design, as the design does not have any architectural composition.

A common factor for design and architecture is that both evolve with development. Some years ago, we would create a rigid structure that would not develop over time because it did not need to. Now, both technical and business requirements change at the speed of the market, so instead of fixing our vision on particular architectural or even specific design decisions, we have to learn to think in terms of evolvable structures and adjust our system step by step. As the system evolves, the architect can learn from developers' feedback and improve his strategy and approach.

To clarify even the slightest misunderstanding, let's look more closely at the differences between the two:

Architecture	Design
High-level components and interactions	Code-level components and interactions
It helps shape the high-level infrastructure of the software	It helps developers achieve implementation of the architectural vision
Main structure	Implementation details
Architectural decisions are harder to change later since they impact more than the coding area	Design decisions are easier to change or correct, as their impact is at the code level
Architectural patterns: patterns that help us shape the high-level structure	Design patterns: patterns that help us create understandable and maintainable code

The subtle distinctions are easy to confuse on the surface, but these differences become evident for significant projects. An extensive system will undoubtedly have many stakeholders, teams, and components.

System design is more about how you implement a specification. A system's plan starts to shine the further that development goes. As the system begins to take shape and increases more strongly.

Summary

Although treated as two different areas, design and architecture are two stages of an application life cycle that work in tandem. As discussed, architecture comes first with a system's high-level structure and relationships, so the necessary experience and overview are required to make the best decisions considering any risks or changes to the requirements.

After the clear architectural direction is established, we move to the next stage: the system design. The system design represents a set of specifications that will support developers in developing the architecture that we have already defined. Software design is concerned more with modules and components, their relationships, and their evolution. It is more about the system's inner workings.

In the next chapter, we will discuss different types of architects and their focuses.

Part 2 – Architect: From Title to Role

In this part of the book, we will focus on the role that has the best overview of an application's architecture: the role of the architect.

This part comprises the following chapters:

- *Chapter 6, Types of Software Architects and Their Focus*
- *Chapter 7, Leveraging Soft Skills*

6

Types of Architects
and Their Focus

Technology is constantly evolving. The product and user expectations evolve, so the architecture grows in complexity too. Many new things will need to be considered all the time when building solid products. Considering this situation, how many types of architects do we have, and how are they different from each other? Why do we need to have them categorized this way and why can't one person take care of everything architecture-related?

The amount of knowledge and expertise needed in software development is immense and it is unrealistic to expect one person to handle it all. This is why, as in other domains, we need specialization, just as we don't have one professor to cover the entire curriculum. So, we need architects with an area of focus and specialization to get the best results. When you focus on too many things at once, it's easy to make mistakes, be less productive, and fail.

While some architects are more strategically focused, others take care of the technical solutions, and the rest link these two areas together, which is crucial, as discussed in previous chapters.

Some of the categories that we are going to discuss in this chapter are the following:

- Enterprise architects

- System architects

- Software architects

- Solution architects

- Application architects

As we can see, each category covers more or less one specific area that is abstract and wide, hence one person can't focus on everything and do it excellently at the same time, and we need this kind of division. Of course, this is just an overview of the various categories of architects. It is essential to understand that each organization can shape the roles within it more specifically. As a result, we will find that some skills and responsibilities are shared.

In this chapter, let's look at each type of architect and get more details about their operating methods.

Enterprise architects

Enterprise architecture is more about operating at a very high level, primarily at a strategic level. Enterprise architecture is more about strategy than code. Therefore, an enterprise architect's role is to create designs at the organization level, analyze what tools are needed at a business level, maintain a close relationship with each department, and get a realistic overview.

Since we are talking about a strategic role that works at the organization level, this role needs a potent combination of soft skills, such as problem-solving, business strategy, and communication, and technical skills, such as cloud computing and strategic development modeling, to name just a few. They need a broad perspective to define the business needs in an ever-changing external environment. This makes them the ones, out of all the types we are going to discuss, that should have the strongest understanding of an organization's strong and weak spots.

When we discuss analytical skills, we also include the ability to understand tech trends and keep track of them. Beyond this, we must follow best practices to correctly decide which ones bring value to what department and introduce them where they are required.

Even though their main focus is not on technical matters, they may sometimes have to deal with a situation where they have to make specific technical decisions or collaborate with solution or software architects. Usually, their focus is on the big picture, and they can influence management to adopt certain new trending technologies to keep up to date and maintain a professional advantage.

Some of the critical responsibilities of the enterprise architect are the following:

- Providing consistency of the product at the design level
- Keeping track of the involved cost and impact of any decision
- Streamlining communication with stakeholders
- Decision-making
- A clear view of the strategy and the ability to communicate it efficiently

In the next section, we will be a bit more specific about the process and discuss the role of a system architect.

System architects

System architecture, also known as software systems, comprises multiple applications using various technologies. Consider an end-to-end software system at a high level and how all levels communicate, integrate, and work together. The system architecture is not only about software but also about understanding how hardware integrates into the bigger picture.

The role of a system architect comprises design, development, and delivery responsibilities. They gather the requirements and objectives and analyze how they can be fulfilled using the best tools, frameworks, and human resources for the job. They are the ones that shape the strategy based on business plans and technical solutions to then present an easily implementable proposal to stakeholders. Part of their responsibility is keeping track of and comparing software trends, hardware trends, and new tools or frameworks that will support long-term business goals.

Let's define some general steps in the work of a software architect:

1. Understanding the business goals and requirements results in a strategy that supports desired goals for all the parties involved (as in, the stakeholders).

2. After creating an overview, it will become more detailed as it considers the technical needs to achieve the outlined goals. At this point, it has to assess the current capacity of the organization and any extra resources potentially needed.

3. The architecture is shaped considering all the gathered information.

4. The software components, hardware components, and their interaction are defined.

5. They ensure that the teams understand the architectural vision and coach them through its implementation.

6. They work closely with the stakeholder to keep them in the loop and decide on any possible changes in direction or risks.

The system architect should have the business-oriented and technical knowledge to keep up with all the aforementioned processes. Soft skills are equally important, as they are they form the common ground with stakeholders. The following table gives you a comparison of the technical and soft skills required:

Technical skills	Soft skills
Knowledge of one or more programming languages in order to support long-term goals strategically	Leadership
Strong knowledge of architectural patterns, quality patterns, and design	Communication
Familiarity with DevOps operations	Negotiation
	Problem-solving

In the next section, we will explain the role of the solution architect and how it differs from the system architect.

Solution architects

When we discuss solution architecture, we discuss an architectural strategy for a set of needs inside the company. This process needs a person that is in charge of the process, so let's discuss what a solution architect is.

As we've discussed before, the role of enterprise architects is a strategic one focused on business-wide directions. It's important to note that the solution architect works on the layer that creates the link between the business goals and technical approaches. This role requires a masterful combination of business and technical requirements to achieve the best possible outcome. This person can be an internal stakeholder, an employee of the company, or a consultant introducing and enforcing the technical vision in the context of a specific solution.

To succeed as a solution architect, there is a solid need to combine both soft and high-level technical skills:

Technical skills	Soft skills
Infrastructure database	Communication
Domain	Resource management
Cloud development	Risk management
System security	Detail-oriented
Network administration	Solution construction and management
DevOps operations	
Business analysis	
Project and product management	

A popular movie states, "with great power comes great responsibility." This is valid in the case of the solution architect. Having so much decisional and strategic power comes with many risks, including the following:

- Failing to keep up to date with the constantly changing and evolving trends. When we discuss the evolution of technology techniques and tools in the last years, I think we can agree that it can become exhausting trying to cover them all without missing important details.

- A huge responsibility in case of failure.

- Failing to keep track of the possible risks and factors affecting the application and devise solutions or ways to avoid these failure scenarios.

- Keeping the stakeholder's needs balanced and finding solutions to satisfy them.

Let's discuss the responsibilities of the application architect.

Application architects

Application architecture describes the general way of working used in business applications. Application architecture is shaped around the application's interactions within the business and its relationship with its users. The application architect has to ensure that the technical quality attributes are implemented within the suite of applications.

As an application architect, you need high-level application development experience and the ability to evaluate business requirements. Therefore, as shown in this table, an application architect must combine tech and soft skills in specific areas:

Technical skills	Soft skills
Taking care of the documentation of all the processes and procedures needed in product development	Leadership, coaching, and interpersonal skills
Keeping track of tech trends and possibly integrating them into the projects wherever they can bring value	Communication and collaboration skills
Keeping track of migrations, integrations, and maintenance	Negotiating skills
Being an active part of the design and mitigating eventual modifications	Analytical and problem-solving skills
Ability to run tests and keep track of performance procedures	Organizational and time management skills

Lastly, we will discuss the role from a perspective we've touched on multiple times before now in the book and draw some conclusions.

Software architects

While software architecture is about a specific software solution composed of structured components, a system architecture is represented by a high-level view of how systems are designed.

A software architect is the one working closest to the development team. A software architect also helps the team understand the vision of what they are building, determine processes and practices, and decide on the right technologies for the team to use. This role is about finding the proper structure for solutions that fit the company's direction and tech possibilities.

The architect's role is the most technical in closely collaborating with teams to develop and implement effective solutions. This high-level role focuses on combining the right technology choices with the design and technical standards to fulfill stakeholders' needs.

Some of the primary responsibilities of this role are the following:

- Recurrent discussions with stakeholders to discuss the evolution of the product, the possibility of any new requirements in the context of the technical solution, and enhancements needed in the process
- Keeping close to the team, explaining the vision, and leading them through the implementation process
- Determining and analyzing the product's proper standards, tools, and processes, considering the needs of stakeholders and business capabilities

- Tailoring the solution to the company's vision and resources
- Staying in the loop of the development in the delivery process

Commonly, software architecture focuses on a specific technical solution. The solution usually follows a pattern that helps keep the quality attributes at a high level.

Although we discussed them separately, it is essential to note that in many companies, especially big companies or complex products, the software architect and the system architect either work together or are represented by the same person.

Summary

The amount of information, skills, and expertise needed in architecture at different levels is hard to be covered by just one person. In this chapter, we discussed the various types of architects. Here's a quick review of them:

- Enterprise architects:

  - No interaction with the code.

  - Focus on the business side.

  - Overall view on the tech trends.

  - Effect on the whole development of the company.

  - Their decisions impact the whole technical context of the company.

  - Communicates technical decisions in the company.

- System architects:

  - Focuses on one system and its inner workings

  - Focused on the technical side and processes of the product

  - Involved in management decisions

  - Overall view on the tech trends

- Software architects:

  - Closest to the technical team, ensuring all solutions are being developed following the architectural vision while keeping track of good practices and good design

  - Coaches the development teams in following the quality attributes

- Solution architects:

  - Involved in business discussions

  - Works with several systems and integrates them where needed

  - Important communication points between different system teams

  - Involved in both business and technical matters

- Application architects:

  - Analysis of business requirements and comes with technical solutions

  - Keeps processes consistent

  - Keeps up with the requirements of stakeholders and translates them into technical solutions

In the next chapter, we discuss soft skills, their importance, and how the lack of soft skills can damage the product even when technical expertise is high.

7
Leveraging Soft Skills

Since I first joined the technical world as an developer and learned the inner workings of its teams, the role of an architect was always presented as someone that had little to no interaction with the development team, someone whose decisions couldn't be challenged, and someone who carried out the essential tasks for the product.

As a junior and in my first project ever, I didn't even get the honor of meeting the architect. I worked on the project for over a year. So, yeah, you can imagine that when I later switched teams, and the architect had the desk closer to mine, I understood the difference between a title and a role.

The role of an architect is to be a leader most of the time and therefore, they have to work on having the best communication skills. They have to know how to shape their speech to be understood by both the technical team and the businesspeople.

In this chapter, we will discuss some of the main areas in which depending on the type of involvement, the architect has the responsibility of bringing about specific results, and how we can improve those results. These are the topics we'll cover in this chapter:

- The role in the team
- Coaching
- Effective communication
- Collaboration
- Stakeholder management
- Decisions and risk management

An architect serves different roles. Next, we will be deciphering what it takes to be an architect.

The role in the team

An architect is not just a person building architecture. We must get away from the mindset of "the architect architects the architecture." I'm not saying that teams shouldn't have someone formally owning the architect's role, but any developer can come up with ideas or insights over time that can impact the current state of architecture.

I found it essential in my journey to look at the architect's role through two lenses: leadership over management and expertise over knowing everything. While the second one will be discussed in the next section, I would like to explore the leadership side of the role here.

There's a difference between management and leadership. Management is about getting stuff done and clearing tasks step by step. Leadership comes with a more human touch. As Simon Sinek defines it, "it's less about what you're doing and more about who you're being. It's how you show up for your people. It's being available to handle the human side of things."

Someone with a better overview, experience in various areas, and insights into functional and non-functional requirements is responsible for the growth of the team around them. An architect should understand that each team member comes with a different level of knowledge, and it is the architect's responsibility once again to ensure a common understanding of the architectural vision. Everybody on the development team needs to see the essence of software architecture and the consequences of not thinking about it before discussing architecture description languages and evaluation methods. The way I see it, even business people or people that manage software teams should understand the essence of software architecture and why its discipline is necessary. I've seen many cases where colleagues that were not that technically minded did not understand the system as a whole but saw it more as a sum of requests and planned specific changes without understanding the level of complexity that certain features or approaches to some features could bring.

When we are constantly chasing deadlines, trying to check metrics, and delivering, sometimes we forget about the people doing the work, the members who make all these things happen. We don't usually talk about the soft side of being a software architect. So, of course, an architect's role is to worry about critical technical decisions. Still, at the same time, a key part of the role is leading, giving the team direction, explaining, influencing, collaborating, and coaching. When we talk about a leadership role, these soft skills are fundamental.

When we discuss their position in the team, an architect's role is mainly concerned with three areas: technical and architectural matters (quality, deployment, monitoring, and processes), team dynamics, and communication with stakeholders. Taking care of these areas means a lot of communication. An architect must bring quality over quantity to whatever they do. They need to handle different communication styles easily: they have to be a strong leader, especially for their team. They have to coach, motivate, and listen, which makes up a large part of their communication skills. Another area is the relationship with the business, decision-making, and planning. They have to be able to provide context and have a strong focus on business when considering the status of the team.

Lastly, they need emotional intelligence to combine describing the technical context, making decisions, and dealing with failure. Business people won't understand the language we use to discuss specialized tools and frameworks with developers. We have to explain technical concepts in ways that they understand and that contribute to the collaborative process efficiently.

Of course, this is an undertaking that requires time and practice.

Coaching

Choosing architects by insisting on technical abilities is not a great way of going about it. Of course, you want leaders with strong technical knowledge, but technical skills are not everything. Technical skills are easier to learn than attitude and emotional intelligence.

We agreed in the previous section that communication is essential. Well, let me tell you that connection is crucial. For my team and me, connecting was a game-changer. That connection is created when you genuinely care for the people around you and when you try to understand and support them in their professional journey.

An architect is not only leading the team but, more importantly, is part of the team. Being a leader means being there with people, showing up for them, and discussing and making decisions together. But at the same time, be a team leader. Am I confusing you? I used to be confused too. This is the real challenge of leading in the tech field – treading the fine line between being part of the team and being aware that the team needs you to lead them. Just to make it more straightforward, let's bear in mind two lessons that I've learned:

- Listen to the team first, then provide your perspective. It might be the result of education or just a lack of self-confidence. Still, I've noticed that when someone in a position of power expresses their opinion first, others don't dare to challenge it or even give their opinion. Try this with your team. By encouraging them to speak up first, you might get some excellent ideas and insights from what is happening in the code base but also on technical matters that you maybe didn't consider.

- On achievements, praise the team. On failures, you own it. When the team does well, delivers on time, or has a successful evolution, the leader will give them all the appreciation, recognize their merits, and promote their success. On the other hand, when things are going bad, the leader must own it. No matter whose fault the failure is, blaming team members is not a leadership move. The leader has to take care of shifting the attention from the problem to the solution. Then, solve the situation inside the team.

Effective communication

This is not an overnight process. It takes time and effort; you won't become a great communicator unless you have some kind of innate emotional intelligence, but for those that find it harder to navigate crucial conversations, you can start by working on your assertiveness, listening skills, and ability to give and receive feedback.

Another essential aspect to remember is that even though you are in a position of power and have to show your strength of character and sound resource management skills, you are also human. There are a lot of areas to cover – soft skills, technical skills, the ever-changing trends, the ever-changing market – and then you also have a personal life. The thing is, don't be afraid to ask your team to help you. Create trust. Be honest and ask for help when you need some or are just looking for inspiration. Build trust, collaborate, and dare to be vulnerable from time to time.

Collaboration

There's a difference between management and leadership. Management is about the tasks and concrete steps to achieving the end goal.

Leadership is about people, who you are and how you get to those people, how to inspire them, and how you show up for them.

An architect should be a leader that has a better overview, experience in diverse areas, and insights into both functional and non-functional requirements in order to contribute to the growth of the team around them. An architect should understand that each team member comes with different levels of knowledge about architecture, as it's their responsibility to ensure common understanding.

Everyone on the development team needs to see the essence of software architecture and the consequences of not thinking about it before they start talking about things such as architecture description languages and evaluation methods. My own experience has empowered me to say that I even see the need for the people that manage the software teams to understand the essence of software architecture and why its discipline is necessary.

We don't usually talk about the soft side of being a software architect. But in the real world, an architect's role is worrying about the important technical decisions and leading, giving the team direction, explaining, influencing, collaborating, and coaching.

We are basically talking about a leadership role. Soft skills are fundamental.

A team with the same view that finds it easy to collaborate is more engaged and delivers quality and quantity.

Therefore, if you ask me, I think an architect should have a software development background. If, as an architect, you don't know and don't understand what is happening in the code base, you might fail to make good decisions. But here is where the misunderstanding is born. Many think that the architect must also be the team's best developer. As we discussed, it is almost impossible to master the whole stack. Still, something more valuable than getting things going is the ability to switch between code and implementation details and the big architectural picture.

Yes, as an architect, you should own best practices, approaches, overviews on design, and patterns that bring the most value to specific technologies and help choose the right one in the project context. But when it comes to keeping an eye on the details of low-level code, I think actual value exists in using the team's technical expertise. The software architect role can sometimes simply be that of another team member. We must create a trustful and collaborative environment where people can express their ideas and expertise.

Stakeholder management

Before we fully understood how vital architecture and its evolution were within a product's life cycle, we felt that architecture wasn't something that teams should consider. Once the AGILE method of doing things gained popularity, how we shaped a system's structure changed. If in most cases, architecture was discussed from the start in the first place and followed carefully during development, things evolved in a more organized direction. The need for change was perceived more and more. Products changed while being developed. There were two main reasons for this:

- The tech stack changes terribly fast. Approaches and tools evolve quickly and we must create the best user experiences and solid systems for our stakeholders.

- Alongside the evolution of the tech stack, requirements also evolved. Users change their minds, the competition in the same market is enormous, and new features appear constantly.

Considering this, we can't discuss an upfront architecture that is mindlessly followed. Creating a system's architecture is an ongoing process and this process needs to be transparent to all the stakeholders to achieve the best results. Generally speaking, stakeholders come in three categories:

- The ones that develop and work for the product.

- The ones that use the product.

- And the third category being even though they are not using or developing the product, they still facilitate some processes that help the development of the product.

We are stakeholders. We don't always know what we want regarding non-functional requirements, other than that if something looks shiny, we want it.

When discussing requirements, there will always be a definitive list of what people want a system to do. Alongside this, a plan will always be nicely split between features, user stories, flows, and tasks. On the other hand, when we try to research the less functional requirements, usually the most known and desirable ones revolve around quality – again, pretty abstract. Some of these given characteristics are more self-explanatory. Still, some requirements are not very well understood and wanted most of the time just because someone has mentioned that "performance" or "flexibility" might be necessary.

When talking about the well-known "quality attributes," everyone wants them all – this list can increase but that doesn't make them all equally important. Some are more relevant and have more weight depending on the context of your system. Please research and understand the quality characteristics that will help your strategy and focus on keeping it as healthy as possible at the beginning of building a system or when extending an existing one.

Decisions and risk management

As business evolves, so does our software, depending on the context and domain. What we need is to think in terms of building tolerance to change within the system. Observe where and what kind of changes appear through iterations. You can expect these changes and be prepared to meet them. Why so much analyzing?

Every time we make a final decision, we also say no to further details we might receive over time, which could help us make more informed decisions.

Making decisions concerning architectural aspects is very sensitive because these decisions have a huge impact. One of the best practices in software development is to avoid making decisions until the very last moment because there is a high level of uncertainty, especially in architecture. This makes the future hard to predict. When things are hard to predict, we tend to speculate. We are aware of this and trying to push the moment of deciding the limit forward is essential to building a system with the capacity to be changed and extended. So, a good strategy to be prepared to commit is gathering feedback (if we are talking about an existing system) but not getting lost in the details, and when that is the case, we need to learn to accept that some of our past decisions were not the best and that we might have to rethink and improve some of them. A better strategy for delaying commitments when developing a complex system is always to have a way out, therefore building while having in mind that you need some capacity to change in the system.

In the spectrum between a dictator and a yes-man, choose to be a leader. A leader knows when to be firm (and has all the arguments to do so) and when to be flexible. This is valid not only in leadership but also in personal development – knowing where to set boundaries.

Decision-making is an essential characteristic of the role, so you can't really afford to flip a coin. An helpful approach to decision-making is the OODA loop. These are the specific steps used in the military regarding the decision-making process under high pressure when situations need rapid and efficient solutions:

1.   Observe – Make sure you see the whole context and have as much information as possible.

2.   Orient – Analyze how the data can help you shape a plan for your problem, situation, or proposal.

3.   Decide – Decide on the direction where you want to act and make a plan

4.   Act – Follow your plan. Engage with your decision and act on it.

This brings us to the end of this chapter.

Summary

Being an architect is not something you simply read about. You can't memorize 10 rules and then be ready to change the world. Most of the time, it is a tedious path with many challenges.

In this chapter, we learned that as an architect, you need to make your influence felt in the team and collaborate with the people that work on the same product as you do. As a role that influences a wide range of stakeholders, you need to learn to communicate effectively and manage the information you get from each to make the best decisions for the product.

Holding a leadership position within the technical field does not spare us from being there for our team, raising our colleagues by giving feedback or mentoring. Maybe one of the ideas we need to get out of our systems is that while you are an engineer or a tech person, you don't need to collaborate or have expertise in working with people. Great teams deliver great products. You can have a group of superstars owning the stack and finding solutions to all complex scenarios. Still, if you can't build a team out of that group, the consequences will be evident in the development of your product.

Discover, learn, and build on your leadership style.

In the next chapter, we will go a bit deeper into how involved an architect should be in the development phase and how we can align on the architectural vision.

Part 3 – From Developer to Architect

By completing this part, you will gain specific skills and a mindset that will significantly help in the process of becoming an architect.

This part comprises the following chapters:

8

Who Codes and Who "Architects"?

Sometimes, when we are in a high-level role with great expectations on our shoulders, it might seem difficult to lean toward someone from the team and ask for an opinion. At the same time, we sometimes give particular importance to some high-level roles or to our tech "heroes", which blocks us from being honest, asking for mentoring or for some clarifications, or giving suggestions when we could contribute. In this chapter, I would like us to open our mind and leave behind all preconceived ideas in order to be able to grow, learn, and make great products that we are proud of.

The architect role is challenging, and the expectation is to have a lot of knowledge and expertise. But the confusion starts here: you don't need to be an expert in all software areas to become an architect. This is an unrealistic expectation. Considering the speed with which the technology stack has evolved in the last decade, there is enormous pressure on architects. Ultimately, it will begin to be seen as a role no one is ever fully prepared for.

A more realistic way to think about this role is to use the experience and expertise of the team while raising team members professionally. Add to this having an overview of software development and communicating your knowledge effectively while being backed up by best practices.

In this chapter, we will cover the following topics:

- The skills of an architect
- Team dynamics
- Strategic thinking
- Pair programming

The skills of an architect

We must note that you don't have to be a god of the technology stack to become an architect. I find it helpful to have a broad perspective on software development, emotional intelligence, leadership skills, and coaching. More specifically, some general skills embody the "architect role".

Comprehend both functional and non-functional requirements. Take a pragmatic view combining what the user/client wants, what are their needs.

In development and architecture, we work on establishing the best solution, but that doesn't mean all risks are removed. You can choose the most remarkable and modern technologies, but the result is damaging when applied in the wrong context. Every technology choice comes with the need for awareness of both costs and advantages. Our job is to research and find the solution that brings the most value in the context of our application and to understand the risks. This also goes for tools/libraries.

Even though we discussed the differences between design and architecture, one of the areas where an architect should have a good understanding is the process of designing software. As we discussed, requirements can change, and risks might appear. It is vital to see how you can fix problems that might arise.

You can think all day about development and creating top-notch architecture; if you don't consider delivery and quality, some challenges and troubles are coming your way. These include code reviews, coding standards, design patterns, and how architecture is understood and implemented.

There was a point in my career when I was working in a team where I did not know whom the architect was, never interacted with them, and never (as a group) did we receive an overview of architecture. It was like this person holding the architect title shaped a structure and handed it to a semi-blindfolded team to develop. We are again underlining the importance of ownership and collaboration throughout the whole evolution and delivery of the system.

As you will see, even though we ask the question of who codes and who architects, the discussion will revolve a lot around collaboration. Let's start with team dynamics.

Team dynamics

How about understanding the system, combined with the collaboration and feedback we discussed, and creating an approach grounded in reality? We need a system that the team understands and knows how to build, and gets why it is essential for it to be made in a certain way. If you implement a middle layer between two parts of your application, ensure that the team understands why you chose to do so if your expectation is for them to make the most of it.

Participating in the development process, either by pair programming, some actual coding, or code reviews, will give you an idea about whether or not your architectural perspectives are grounded in reality. The sooner you have this kind of feedback, a developer's perspective, and an understanding of the pains of working in certain areas, the sooner you can ensure that you work on the evolution of an architecture that is implemented in real-life scenarios and real people. Besides this, being an actual part of the team will build better collaboration and trust in the group. When we don't collaborate, we don't have enough information, and when we don't, we make assumptions. Clarifying these assumptions by discussing actual data can spare us some unpleasant surprises. As Simon Brown (author of *Software Architecture for Developers* and the creator of the C4 software architecture model) nicely put it, the whole process should be like pair programming – he just named it in a highly self-explanatory way: pair architecting. Everyone in the team has a perspective and knowledge that might be missing in the decision process. So why ignore it?

An architect should come from a software development background and know and understand what is happening in the code base to make the best decisions. But here is where confusion is born: many think that the architect is also the best developer on the team. I would say that they need the ability to switch between code details and the big picture quickly. But it is not always possible for one person to know everything or own the entire technical stack. As an architect, you should own best practices, approaches, and overviews on designs and patterns that bring more value to some technologies or help choose the right one in the project context when it comes to keeping an eye on details of low-level code. I think actual value exists in using the team's technical expertise. The software architect role can sometimes be another team member, even for an idea. We must create a trustful and collaborative environment where people can express their ideas and expertise.

Strategic thinking

Continuing the idea that not everything labeled as quality is what you need, I would like to discuss best practices. Again, weigh the complexity of your system, the time you invest in some "best practices" versus the advantages they bring, the time you have to invest versus the time it saves, and the constraints of your environment.

Principles, of course, were defined for a good reason after trying and failing in specific scenarios, but that doesn't mean that they are applicable in all systems. When the essential principles are clear and well-weighted, everyone in the team should be aware of them and ensure everyone is going in the same direction and is on the same page. Maybe you will find it hard to decide on that list of principles because the system's context is sometimes too complex and hard to follow up in the smallest details. The feedback from the team will help you as an architect determine whether some principles were applicable or not so you can make better decisions in this area later.

I believe that making coding part of your role as an architect is a game-changer. I have worked in teams where the architect opened the IDE and started coding, and I've worked in teams where the architect was just a title – I almost had no idea who that was, and only when I wanted to make an impactful change I had the honor to meet them. What I felt in the first case was engagement with the team and decisions, understanding the reality of the code base and the way the development team was consulted, and I got the chance to know how those decisions impact other areas, how higher-level structures interact, and how our work as developers affects the whole system. It was a game-changer. It created the feeling that we built something extraordinary, and we did. For the second example, unfortunately, the result was a confused and frustrated team because many issues surfaced when different components were integrated. I'm not saying that the architect should take tasks from the board, but being an integral part of the team is vital because of the following:

- As an architect, you better understand the application/components/code base context from a developer's perspective and make more informed, realistic decisions.

- The team will understand the impact and importance of their work and trust you more.

From what we've discussed, maybe with some exceptions, architecture is a part of the development process, a part that is later taken over and implemented by the team. Architecture is not about forgetting implementation details and getting drowned in abstractions but keeping them balanced. The real challenge is knowing when to move slightly from one to the other.

Software architecture is all about understanding how the system works as a whole. Going from contributing to the architecture to being responsible and making decisions to grow a product is a process that has, as a first step, being honest about the level of experience that we have and what areas we need to focus on to go to the next level.

Pair programming

Having strong technical skills does not make you an architect. As an architect, your time spent coding will be limited, so the time invested in your coding skills will also become less and less. But this doesn't mean there are no ways of keeping in touch with the code base. You might not have time to take a task and start working on it, but you can use some of the following approaches at any time:

- **Change of roles**: An excellent way to keep connected with the team and the code base is to consult the team about certain architectural decisions. Besides the feeling of being involved in the process and learning from you as an architect, you can also see what is implementable and why. You can create architectural katas where you can take a brand-new scenario for a problem and brainstorm what architectural approach can be used. This is a great way to create the space to experiment with future architects.

- **Specific ownership of complex features**: You can, from time to time, challenge seniors from your team to take ownership of a particular feature. This way, you can keep connected to the product's development status directly via the one responsible.

- **Pair programming/pair architecting**: You can add on more complex features and do some pair programming. At the same time, you can ask colleagues from the team to give you their perspectives on architecture.

- **Code reviews**: You can look at the pull requests and see how things are going. You don't have to go into detail, but you can spot patterns and see the areas where some knowledge sharing might be needed.

- **Architecture unit tests**: There are tools such as ArchUnit, SonarQube, or SIGRID that can give you feedback on the state of your architectural approach and how aligned your code is with the best practices you have in the team.

- **Quality gates**: Doing automatic checks at build time and release is helpful for the team and the architect. This way, you ensure that the product is quality-oriented, and if there are some faults, you can spot them immediately.

At some point, there might be members in the team that become better at some technical tasks than you are. Again, it is not your technical skills that make you an architect. This mindset will only increase your impostor syndrome and lead you to make many wrong decisions. Having a technical leadership role and less time to invest in your technical skills will sometimes make you feel like you don't deserve the position anymore. There might be members in the team that have more time to dive into the technical debt of your application. As an architect, you must learn to control these feelings and see the end goal. Don't be afraid to use the team's expertise. This way, the team will trust you, and you will create a connection with them and get better feedback.

Summary

We must be aware of the differences that help us evolve, not that divide us. As a programmer, your constant focus is on details, while architects focus most of their time on the whole picture. Most of the time, architects make decisions that programmers have to live with. There is always context to change the perspective and evolve from your level. You never know where your next definitory learning experience will come from.

In the last chapter, we will draw some conclusions and learn about mastery in the software development area.

9
Break the Rules

At this point in the book, you might either find yourself being in a very healthy environment and team and feel validated in your practices, or you might feel that there's a lot of work to do in your context, group, or role, and you don't know where to start. Next up, we will discuss some ideas that might give you a refreshing direction:

- Why is it essential to have a mentor?
- How can you become a craftsman?

After everything we've discussed, one thing is clear: knowing and using best practices is crucial. It is essential to use them in your products and create some rules. However, please don't obsess over them. Keep in mind that you work in real life and in diverse situations. I've been there, doing my best to keep my team engaged and follow coding guidelines. Then we had to prioritize functionality because the business side was okay with skipping an increment of our technical best practices to deliver something as soon as possible. It was not okay, and I was unhappy with the compromise, but looking back, it was a matter of balance because we found a way of getting good code in the end.

Don't focus obsessively on aesthetics. Focus on functionality and quality attributes. Remember that you can have the best product from a technical perspective, strictly following all the rules and best practices, but if that slows you down or becomes a stumbling block, you might want to reconsider your way of doing things.

I believe that even though we can work in distributed teams with clearly defined roles, we should never limit ourselves to the comfort zone of the task at hand. We should be curious and eager to understand what we are building. Always be motivated to grow and find ways of improving your work.

A slight improvement at the code level with the aim of supporting the system's architecture or design will have a considerable impact over time.

So, even if there is a fine line between software development and software architecture, that line should be crossed from time to time to bring a fresh change of perspective. This is valid on both sides, for the architect and the developer. I believe we need to bring system architecture closer to the development team and make it more approachable.

Why is it essential to have a mentor?

Want to become an architect? Read what comes next. Just looking to be a better professional? Also consider the following information.

If you want to start to grow toward an architect career or try to understand the architectural perspective and take your skills to the next level, you can start by taking on more challenging and diverse projects. If you don't know where to start, seek a mentor – someone that can help you shape a direction for your professional goals. Create a learning opportunity from every task and extend your technical skills in different areas. You need an overview to be a good architect and make the right decision.

In the meantime, don't forget about soft skills. There is no use in being the best architect if your team does not understand your perspective. Take responsibility and learn to work with other people.

How can you become a craftsman?

The term "software craftsmanship" comes from the Agile Manifesto. If you are at the beginning of discovering this approach, it may be handy to read Sandro Mancuso's book, *The Software Craftsman: Professionalism, Pragmatism, Pride*, just to have a clear and smooth start.

The software craftsmanship movement revolves around becoming a software professional who, through practice, constant development, and sustained attention to detail and best practices, can achieve mastery in their work and take their work to the level of art. This approach's vital characteristic is understanding that any process takes time. If you have a hard time finding a direction in your career or don't know where to start, this mindset will open some perspectives for you.

The manifesto for software craftsmanship states the following:

"As aspiring Software Craftsmen we are raising the bar of professional software development by practicing it and helping others learn the craft. Through this work we have come to value:

- *Not only working software, but also well-crafted software*

- *Not only responding to change, but also steadily adding value*

- *Not only individuals and interactions, but also a community of professionals*

- *Not only customer collaboration, but also productive partnerships*

- *That is, in pursuit of the items on the left we have found the items on the right to be indispensable.*

- *If and when is useful to create a pathway"*

There is no exact path to becoming an architect or to understanding architecture. The secret is that there is no secret way of becoming good. It is about taking on challenges, investing in yourself, keeping close to people who you want to be like and inspire you, and putting in the extra effort to achieve your goals.

One of the most exciting exercises I have done lately to understand team dynamics within architecture is to create analogies between buildings and software architecture. While doing this and having some very insightful discussions with a friend who is an architecture graduate, I discovered this concept that works very well in software architecture: transpositioning. The idea states that *"by releasing ourselves from disciplinary conventions for a short period of time, we can foster a greater sense of possibility, free ourselves from habitual thinking, and build empathy for others involved in the process."* (`https://snohetta.com/process/transpositioning`). This way, we discuss the problem from an authentic and personal point of view rather than using theoretical methods. Instead of fitting an individual into the group's philosophy, it is essential to benefit from each individual's background and personality to shape the dynamic of the group.

The important thing we can learn from this example is that we are so caught up in our ways of doing things that we often don't see other perspectives. For an industry that is evolving so fast, we sometimes tend stick tightly to fixed processes and practices.

It may be the result of many challenging experiences, but I believe in the vitality of every software team considering software architecture. Failing to do this leads to inconsistencies, integration issues, hard-to-understand codebases, and many quality attributes becoming harder to maintain and grow as the system evolves. On the other hand, teams accumulate a lot of frustration, and developers cannot grow as professionals in a healthy environment. This is a matter of technical leadership. Encourage collaboration, stay present around the coding process, and coach and develop the team.

Summary

All in all, it is helpful to note that to become great leaders, we also have to see what our own characteristics are and what we are best at. We must know ourselves, be willing to understand others, and start building with the information we gather from the books we read, from the experiences of others, and the projects we work with.

I'll sum up by leaving you with two ideas: for developers, a concept called **generative resistance** states that good ideas do not come if everyone agrees on everything or has the same experiences. Be open and confident enough to give feedback to, challenge, and collaborate with the decisions of your technical leader and architect when you are sure your perspective can bring value. At the same time, ask, research, and be curious.

On the other side, for our architects: try deciding on and creating team dynamics regarding technical matters and decisions that make the team feel that great ideas result from the group. Bet on shared thinking for great ideas, and you will witness a shift. You don't have to take my word for it. Go ahead and try and let me know how it goes.

Index

Packt.com

Subscribe to our online digital library for full access to over 7,000 books and videos, as well as industry leading tools to help you plan your personal development and advance your career. For more information, please visit our website.

Why subscribe?

- Spend less time learning and more time coding with practical eBooks and Videos from over 4,000 industry professionals

- Improve your learning with Skill Plans built especially for you

- Get a free eBook or video every month

- Fully searchable for easy access to vital information

- Copy and paste, print, and bookmark content

Did you know that Packt offers eBook versions of every book published, with PDF and ePub files available? You can upgrade to the eBook version at packt.com and as a print book customer, you are entitled to a discount on the eBook copy. Get in touch with us at customercare@packtpub.com for more details.

At www.packt.com, you can also read a collection of free technical articles, sign up for a range of free newsletters, and receive exclusive discounts and offers on Packt books and eBooks.

Other Books You May Enjoy

If you enjoyed this book, you may be interested in these other books by Packt:

Clean Code in JavaScript

James Padolsey

ISBN: 978-1-789-95764-8

- Understand the true purpose of code and the problems it solves for your end-users and colleagues
- Discover the tenets and enemies of clean code considering the effects of cultural and syntactic conventions.
- Use modern JavaScript syntax and design patterns to craft intuitive abstractions
- Express the behavior of your code both within tests and via various forms of documentation.

Software Architect's Handbook

Joseph Ingeno

ISBN: 978-1-788-62406-0

- Design software architectures using patterns and best practices

- Explore the different considerations for designing software architecture

- Discover what it takes to continuously improve as a software architect

- Create loosely coupled systems that can support change.

- Understand DevOps and how it affects software architecture

Packt is searching for authors like you

If you're interested in becoming an author for Packt, please visit `authors.packtpub.com` and apply today. We have worked with thousands of developers and tech professionals, just like you, to help them share their insight with the global tech community. You can make a general application, apply for a specific hot topic that we are recruiting an author for, or submit your own idea.

Share Your Thoughts

Now you've finished *Software Architecture for Web Developers*, we'd love to hear your thoughts! Scan the QR code below to go straight to the Amazon review page for this book and share your feedback or leave a review on the site that you purchased it from.

`https://packt.link/r/1803237910`

Your review is important to us and the tech community and will help us make sure we're delivering excellent quality content.

Made in the USA
Las Vegas, NV
05 May 2023

71595549R00066